GRAPHIC LIBRARY

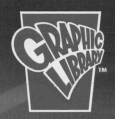

GRAPHIC SCIENCE

A CRASH COURSE IN FORCES AND MOTION

WITH MAX AXIOM SUPER SCIENTIST

An Augmented Reading Science Experience

by Emily Sohn | illustrated by Steve Erwin and Charles Barnett III

Consultant:
Dr. Ronald Browne, Associate Professor of Elementary Education
Minnesota State University, Mankato

CAPSTONE PRESS
a capstone imprint

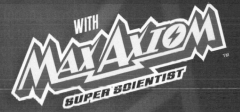

Graphic Library is published by Capstone Press,
1710 Roe Crest Drive, North Mankato, Minnesota 56003.
www.mycapstone.com

Library of Congress Cataloging-in-Publication Data is available on the Library of Congress website.
ISBN: 978-1-5435-2945-6 (library binding)
ISBN: 978-1-5435-2956-2 (paperback)
ISBN: 978-1-5435-2966-1 (eBook PDF)

Summary: In graphic novel format, follows the adventures of Max Axiom as he explains the science behind forces and motion.

Art Director and Designer
Bob Lentz and Thomas Emery

Colorist
Matt Webb

Cover Artist
Tod Smith

Editor
Donald Lemke

Photo Credits
Capstone Studio/Karon Dubke: 29; Library of Congress: 7; NASA/JPL: 13

Download the Capstone 4D app!

- Ask an adult to download the Capstone 4D app.
- Scan the cover and stars inside the book for additional content.

When you scan a spread, you'll find fun extra stuff to go with this book! You can also find these things on the web at www.capstone4D.com using the password: force.29456

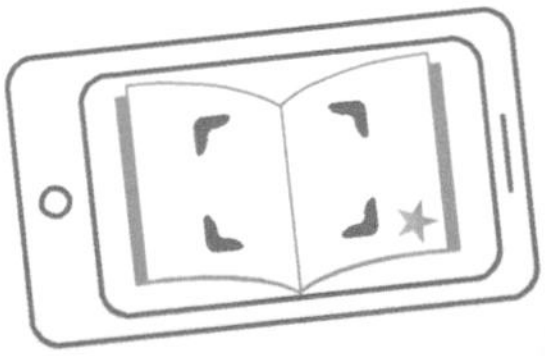

Printed in the United States 4931

TABLE OF CONTENTS

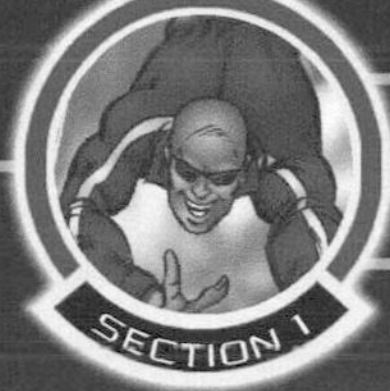
SECTION 1

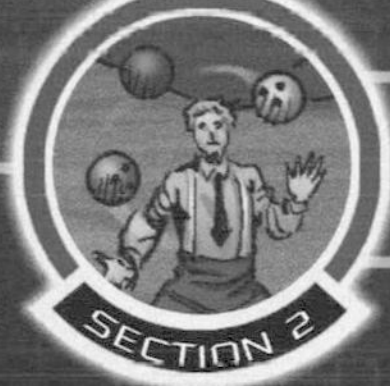
SECTION 2

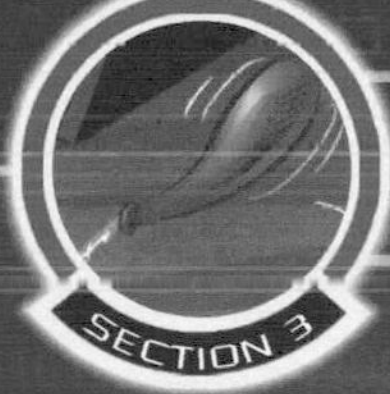
SECTION 3

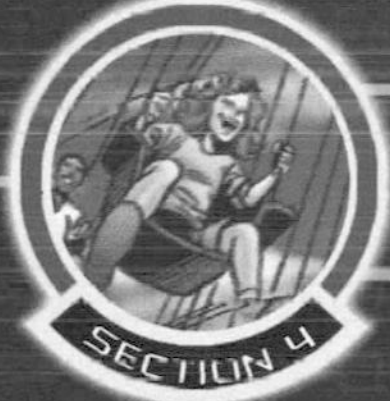
SECTION 4

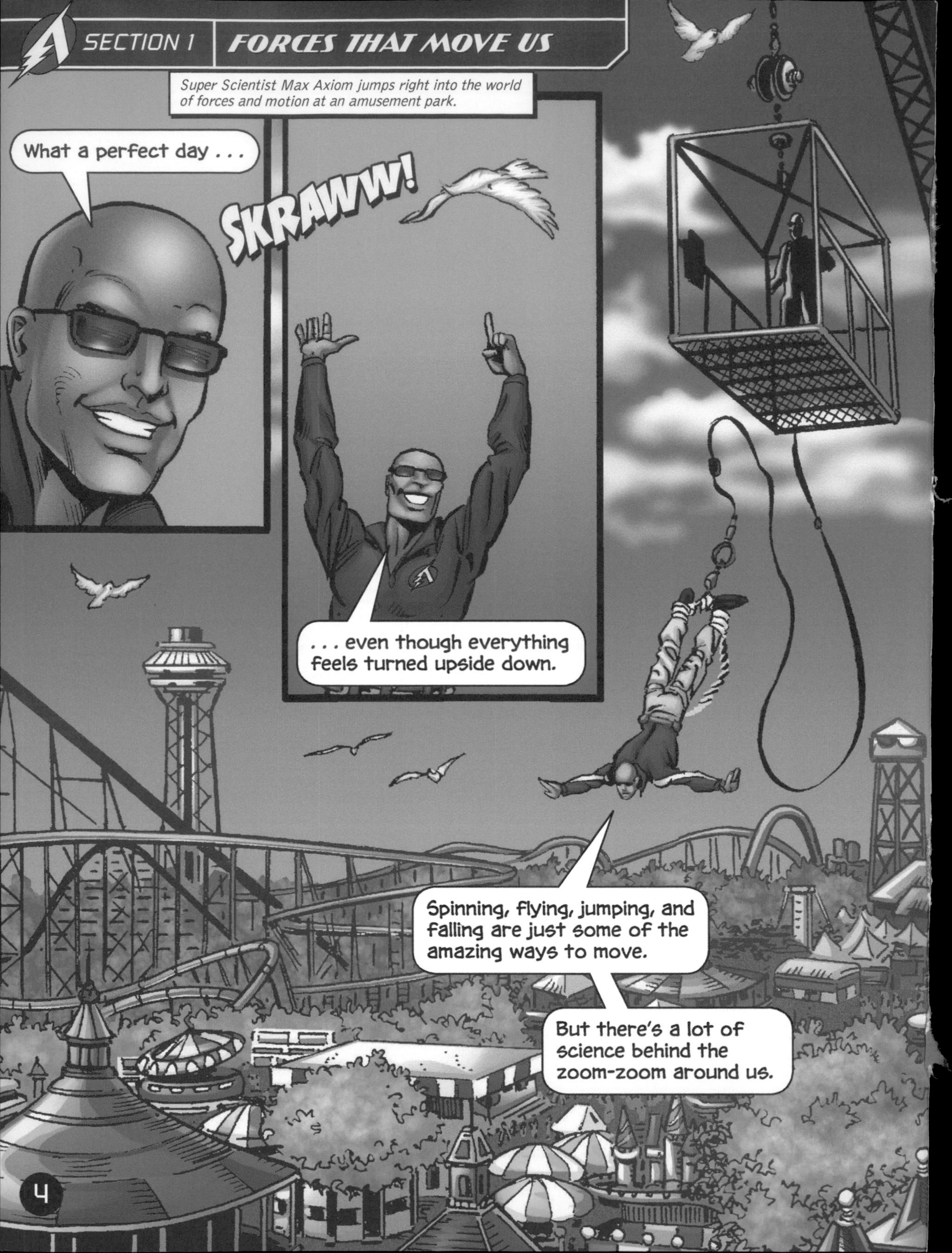

Super Scientist Max Axiom jumps right into the world of forces and motion at an amusement park.
What a perfect day . . .
SKRAWW!
. . . even though everything feels turned upside down.
Spinning, flying, jumping, and falling are just some of the amazing ways to move.
But there's a lot of science behind the zoom-zoom around us.

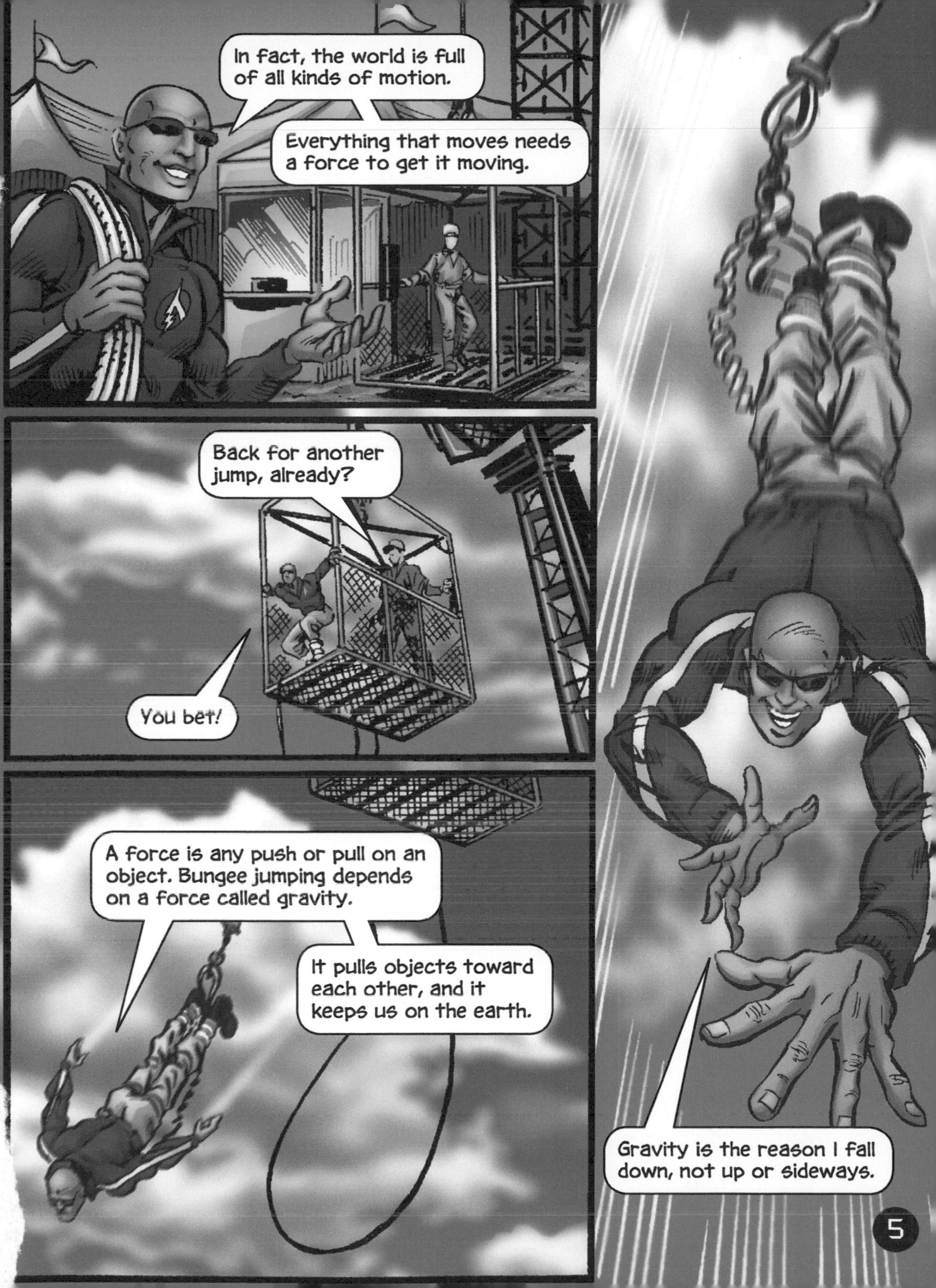
In fact, the world is full of all kinds of motion.
Everything that moves needs a force to get it moving.
Back for another jump, already?
You bet!
A force is any push or pull on an object. Bungee jumping depends on a force called gravity.
It pulls objects toward each other, and it keeps us on the earth.
Gravity is the reason I fall down, not up or sideways.

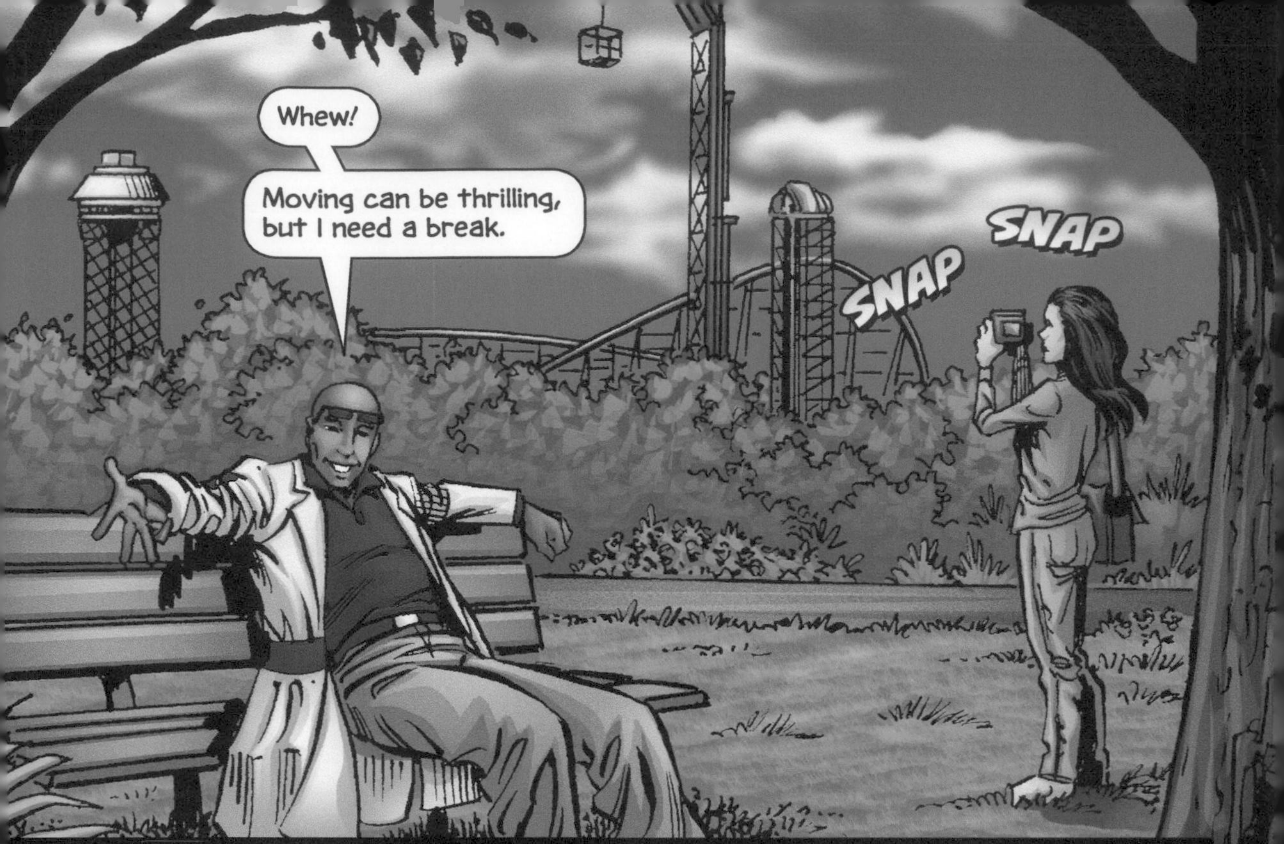
Whew!
Moving can be thrilling, but I need a break.
SNAP
SNAP

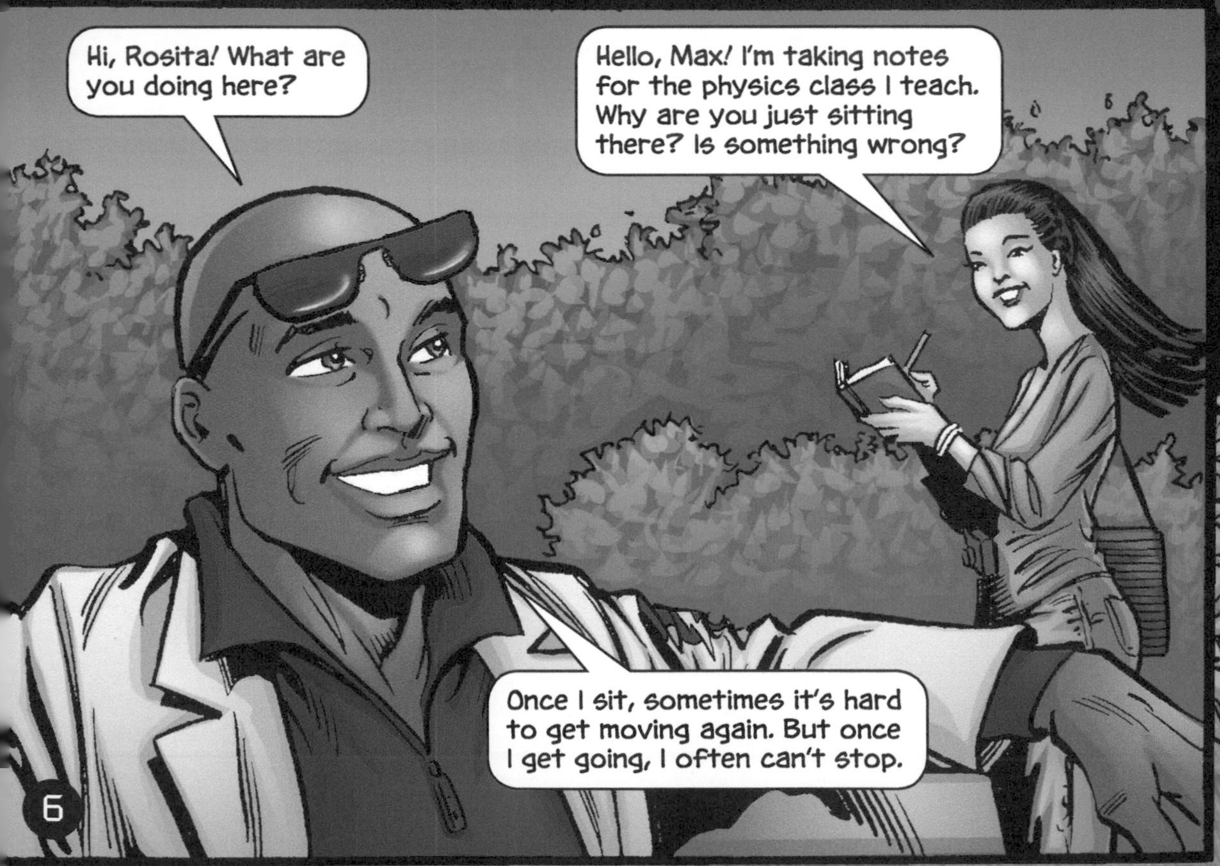
Hi, Rosita! What are you doing here?
Hello, Max! I'm taking notes for the physics class I teach. Why are you just sitting there? Is something wrong?
Once I sit, sometimes it's hard to get moving again. But once I get going, I often can't stop.

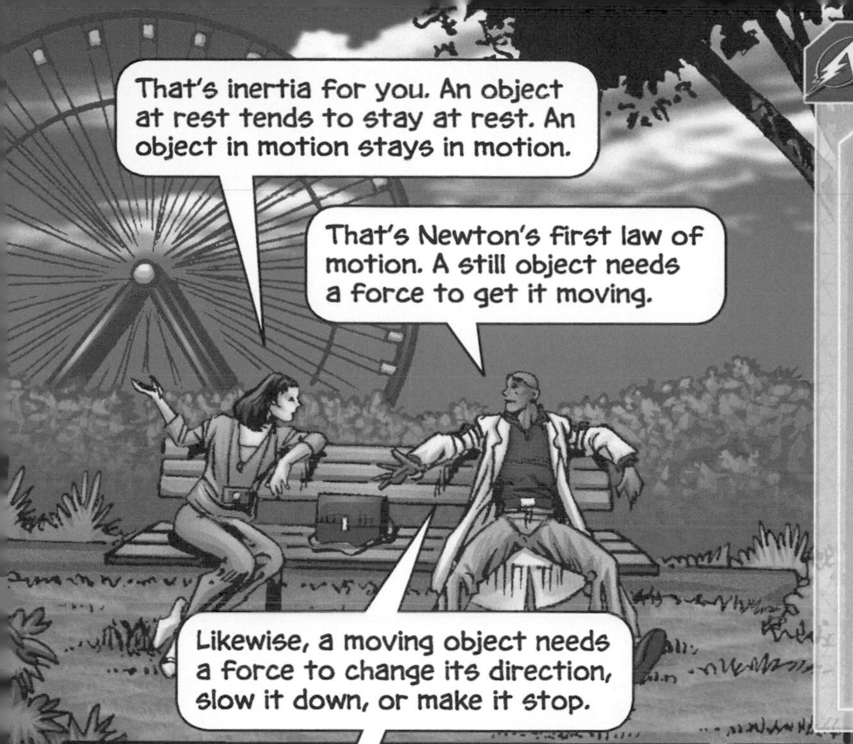
That's inertia for you. An object at rest tends to stay at rest. An object in motion stays in motion.
That's Newton's first law of motion. A still object needs a force to get it moving.
Likewise, a moving object needs a force to change its direction, slow it down, or make it stop.

ISAAC NEWTON

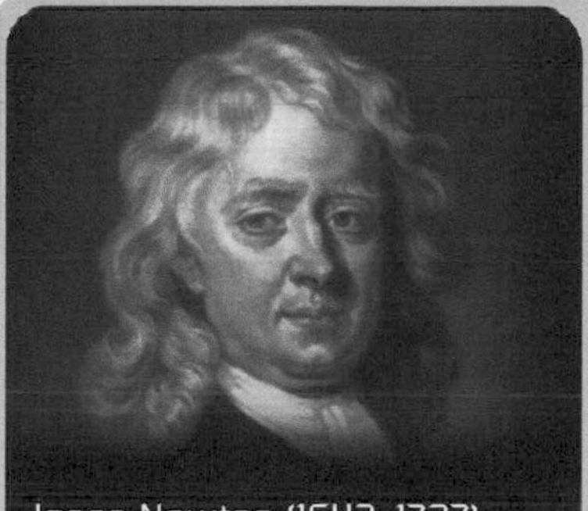

Isaac Newton (1643–1727) was the first person to realize that certain laws of nature explained all motion on Earth and in space. He also was the first to explain the idea of gravity.

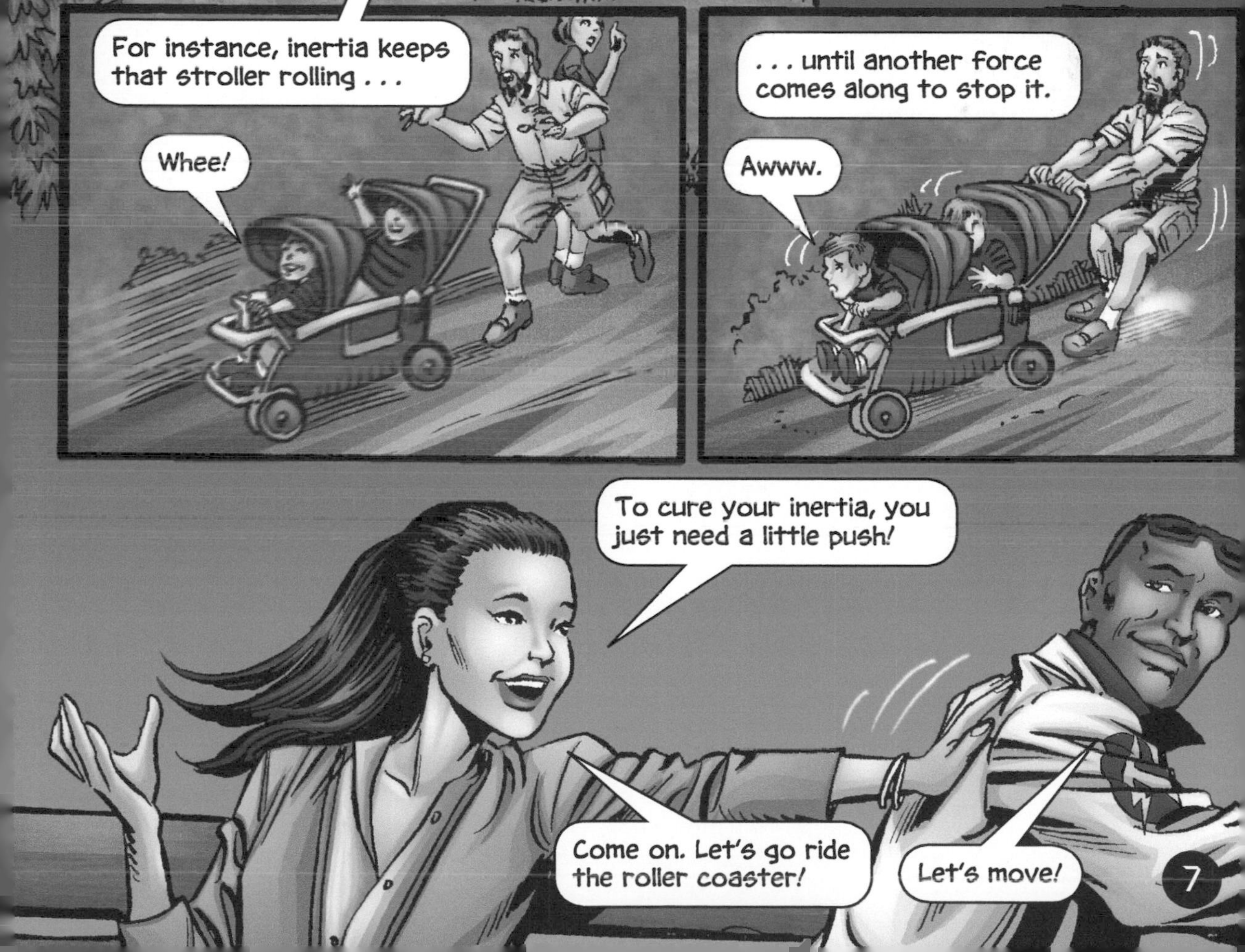
For instance, inertia keeps that stroller rolling . . .
Whee!
. . . until another force comes along to stop it.
Awww.
To cure your inertia, you just need a little push!
Come on. Let's go ride the roller coaster!
Let's move!

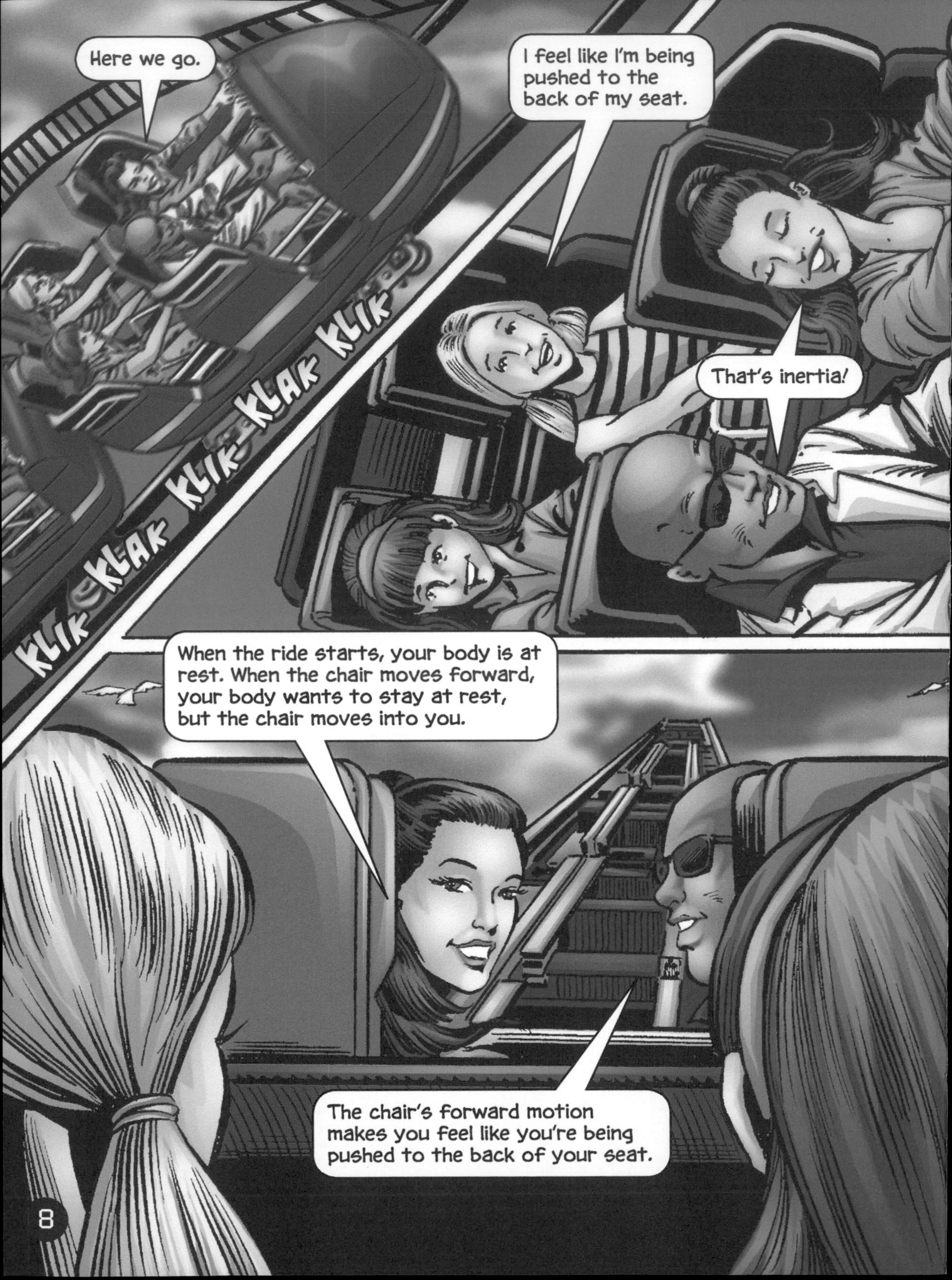
Here we go.
KLIK KLAK KLIK KLIK KLAK KLIK
I feel like I'm being pushed to the back of my seat.
That's inertia!
When the ride starts, your body is at rest. When the chair moves forward, your body wants to stay at rest, but the chair moves into you.
The chair's forward motion makes you feel like you're being pushed to the back of your seat.

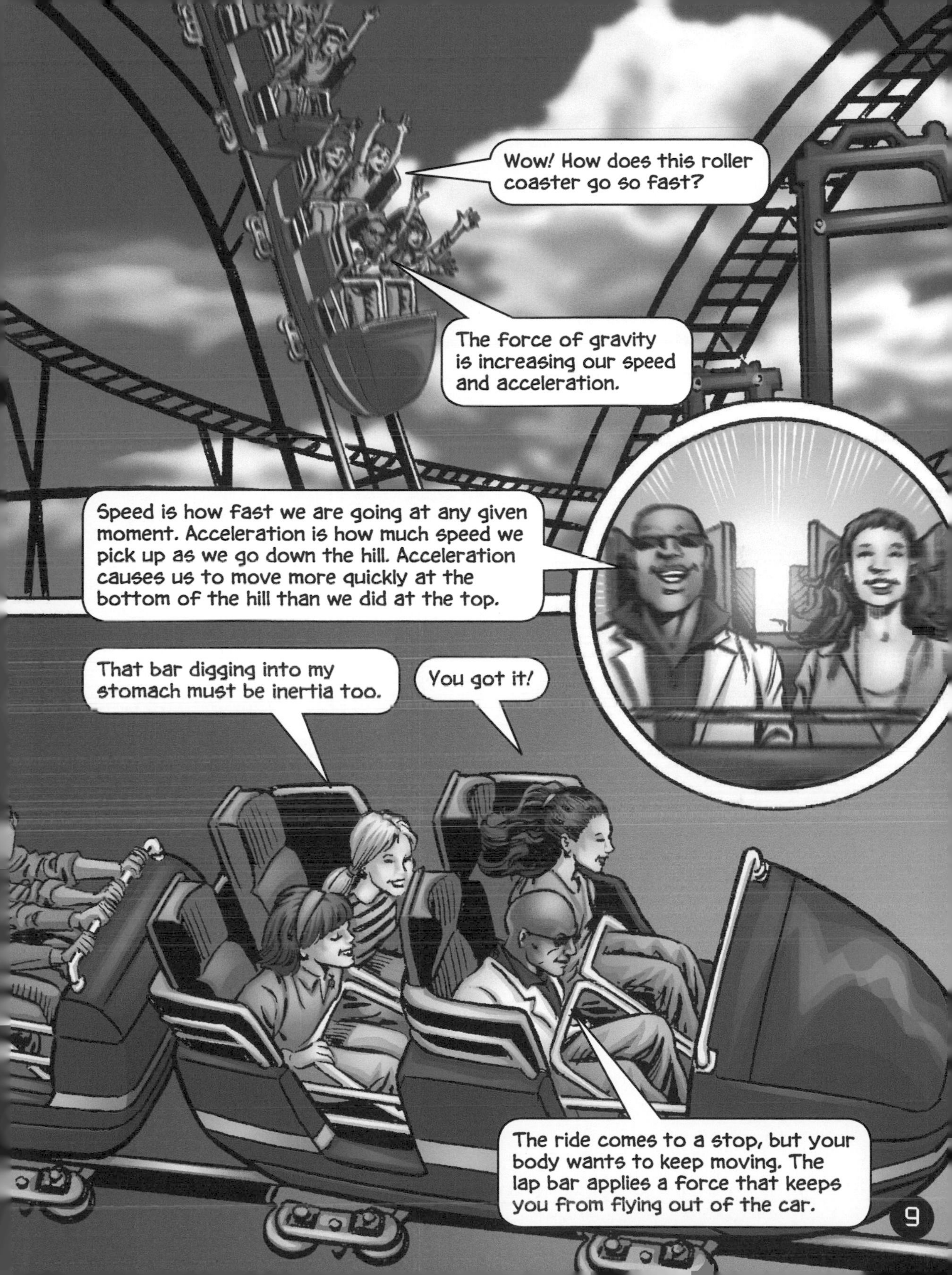
Wow! How does this roller coaster go so fast?
The force of gravity is increasing our speed and acceleration.
Speed is how fast we are going at any given moment. Acceleration is how much speed we pick up as we go down the hill. Acceleration causes us to move more quickly at the bottom of the hill than we did at the top.
That bar digging into my stomach must be inertia too.
You got it!
The ride comes to a stop, but your body wants to keep moving. The lap bar applies a force that keeps you from flying out of the car.

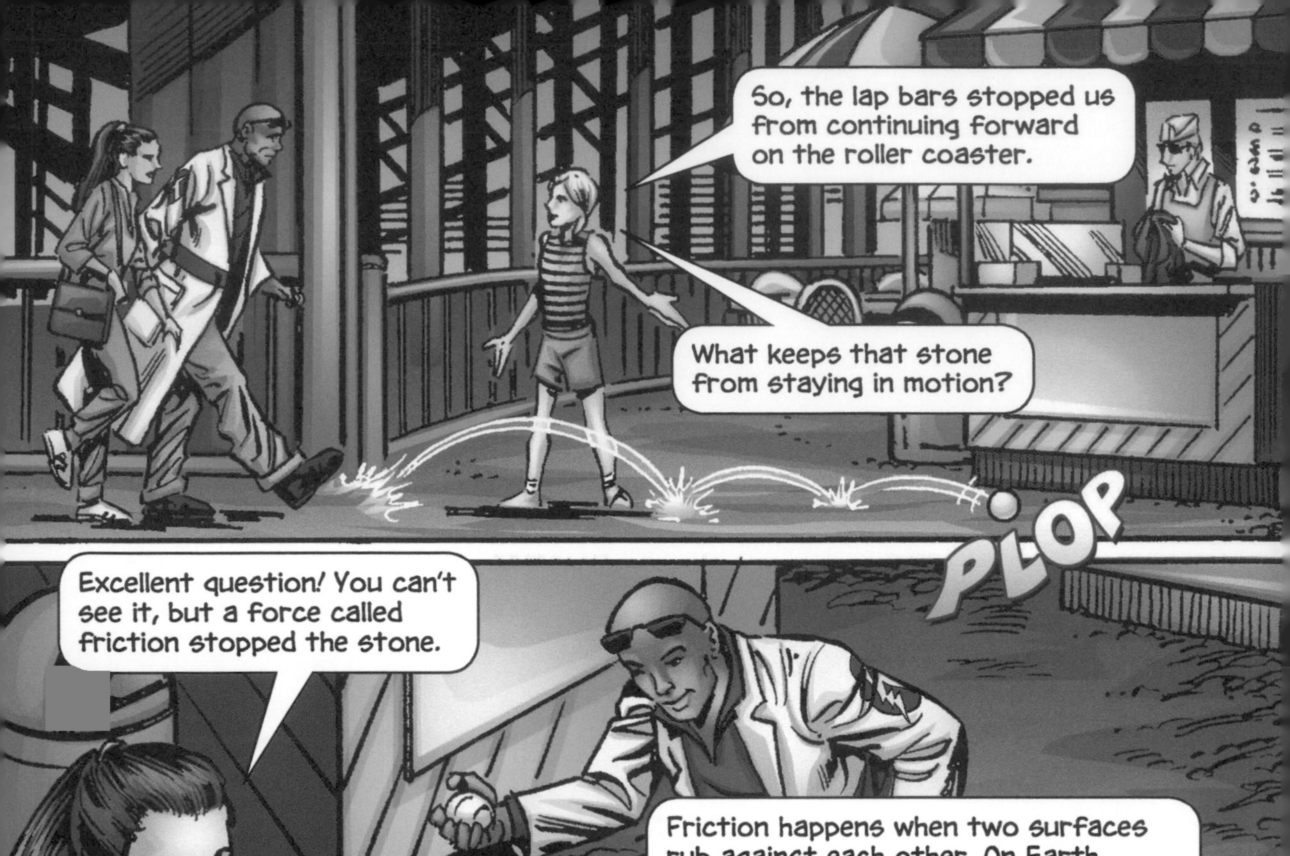
So, the lap bars stopped us from continuing forward on the roller coaster.
What keeps that stone from staying in motion?
PLOP
Excellent question! You can't see it, but a force called friction stopped the stone.
Friction happens when two surfaces rub against each other. On Earth, gravity and friction work together to slow things down and make them stop.

FRICTION IN SPACE

ACCESS GRANTED: MAX AXIOM

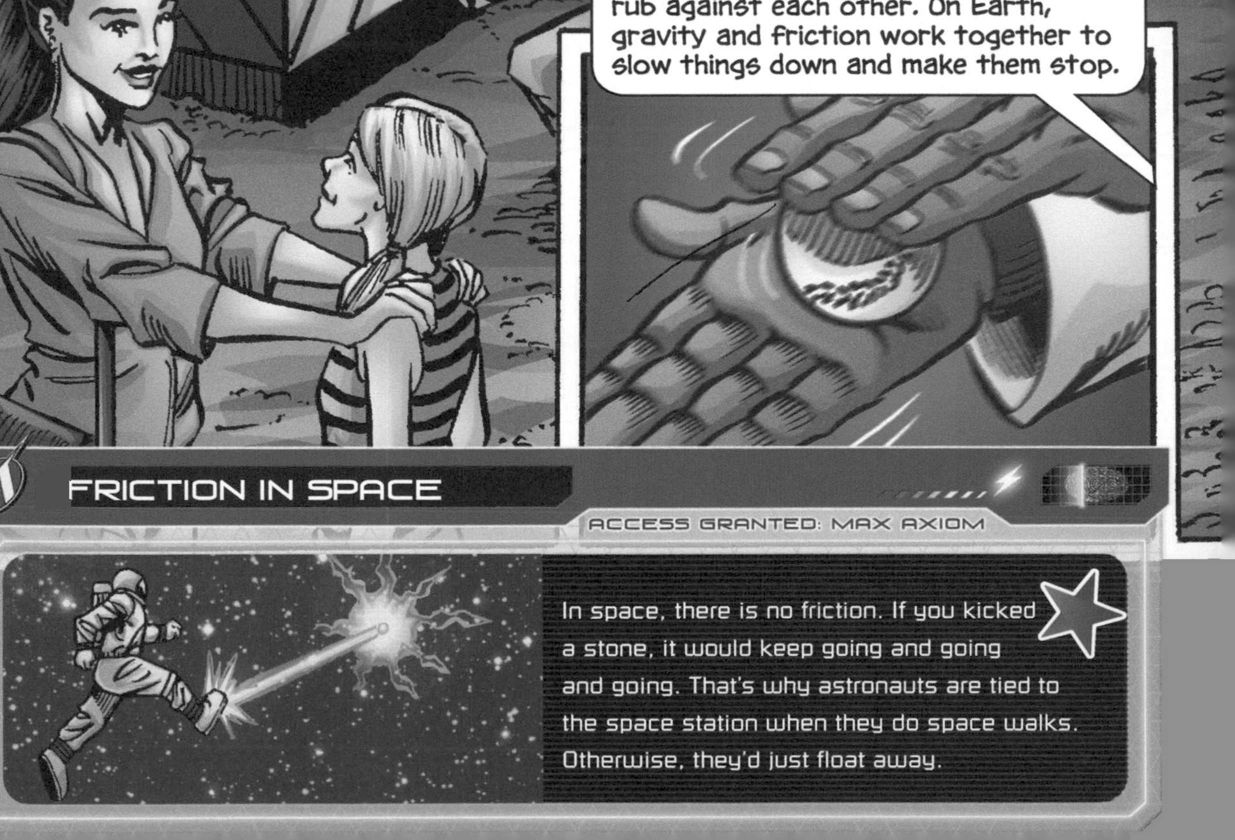

In space, there is no friction. If you kicked a stone, it would keep going and going and going. That's why astronauts are tied to the space station when they do space walks. Otherwise, they'd just float away.

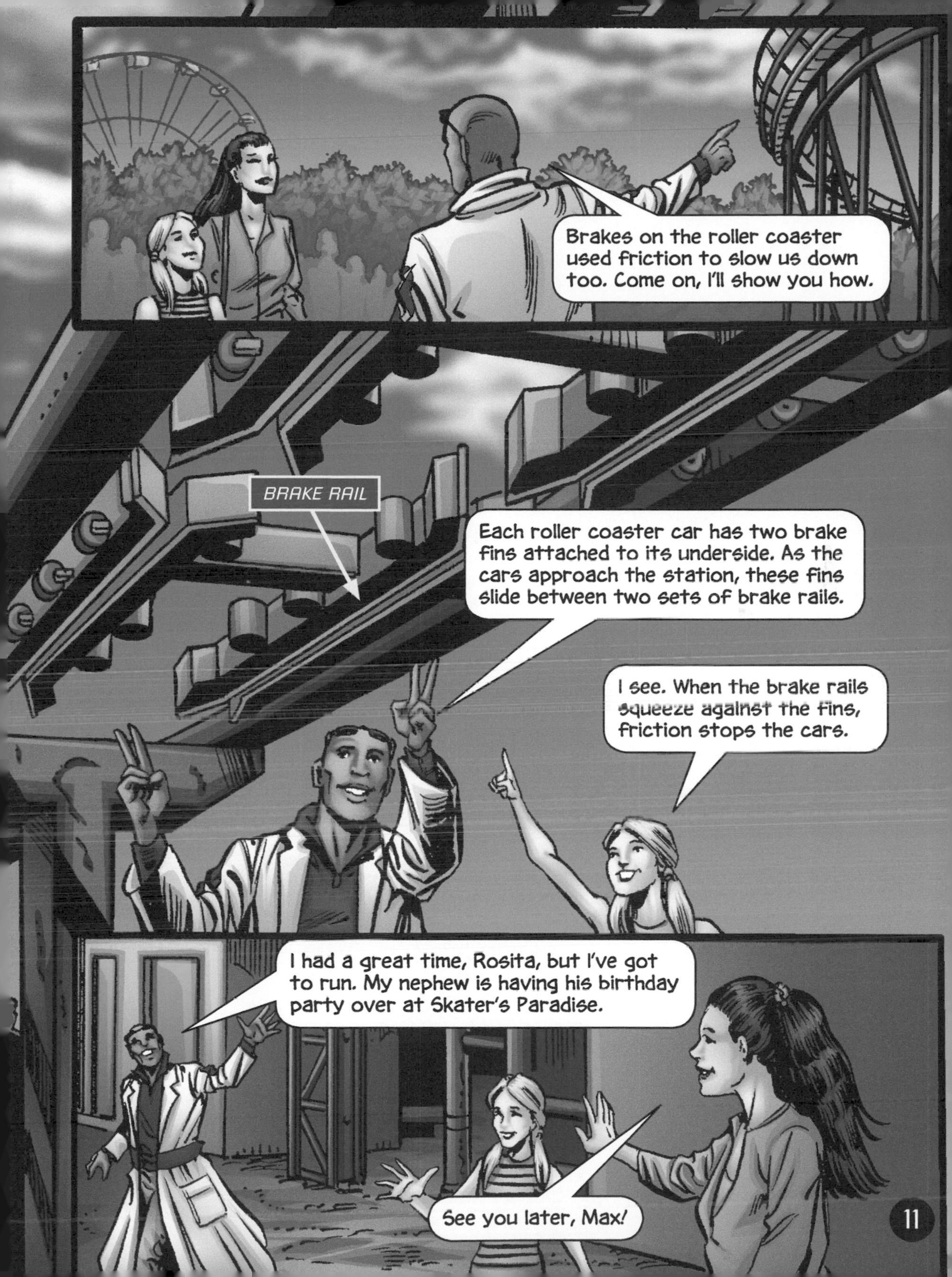
Brakes on the roller coaster used friction to slow us down too. Come on, I'll show you how.
BRAKE RAIL
Each roller coaster car has two brake fins attached to its underside. As the cars approach the station, these fins slide between two sets of brake rails.
I see. When the brake rails squeeze against the fins, friction stops the cars.
I had a great time, Rosita, but I've got to run. My nephew is having his birthday party over at Skater's Paradise.
See you later, Max!

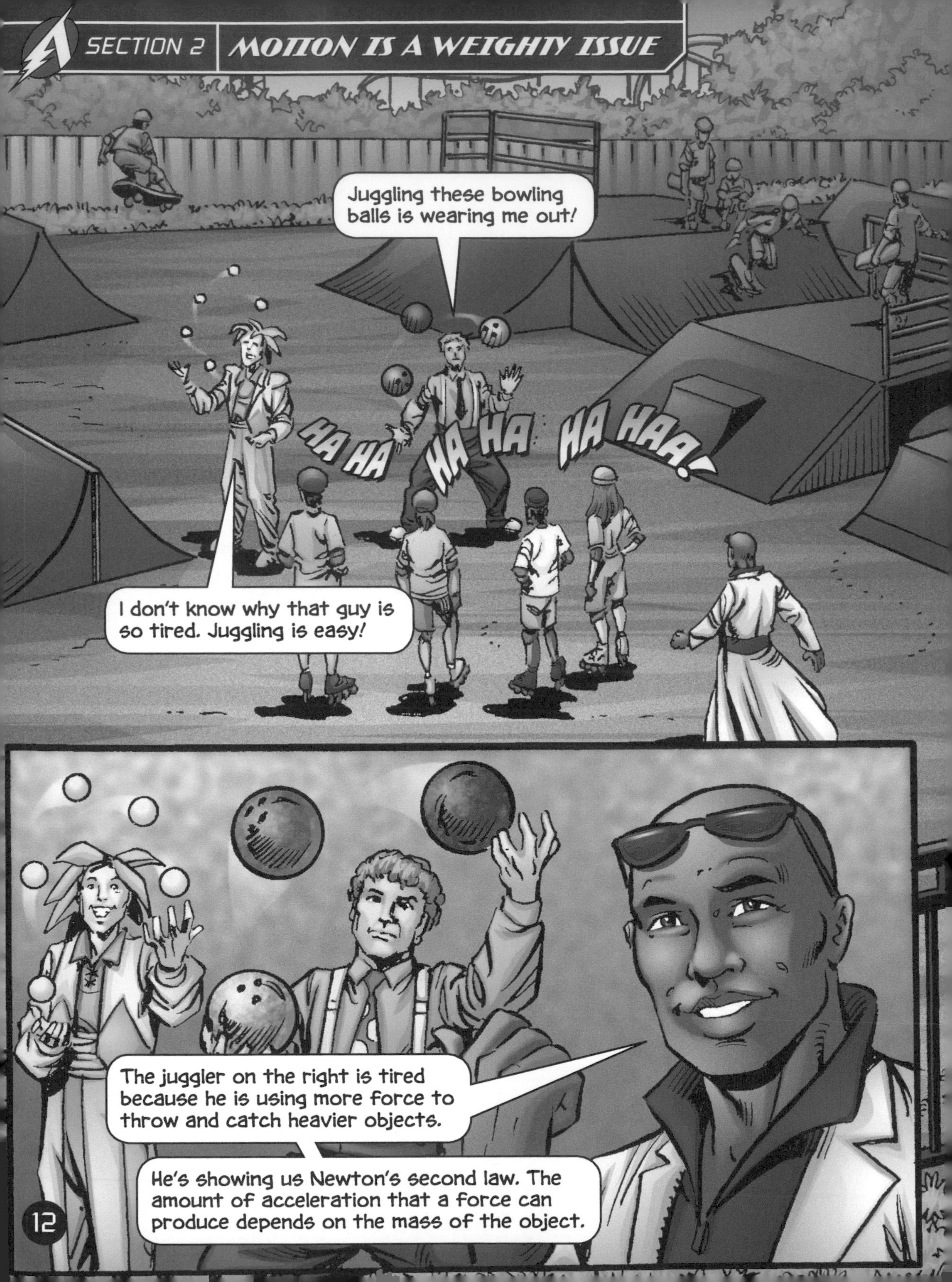
Juggling these bowling balls is wearing me out!
HA HA HA HA HA HAA!
I don't know why that guy is so tired. Juggling is easy!
The juggler on the right is tired because he is using more force to throw and catch heavier objects.
He's showing us Newton's second law. The amount of acceleration that a force can produce depends on the mass of the object.

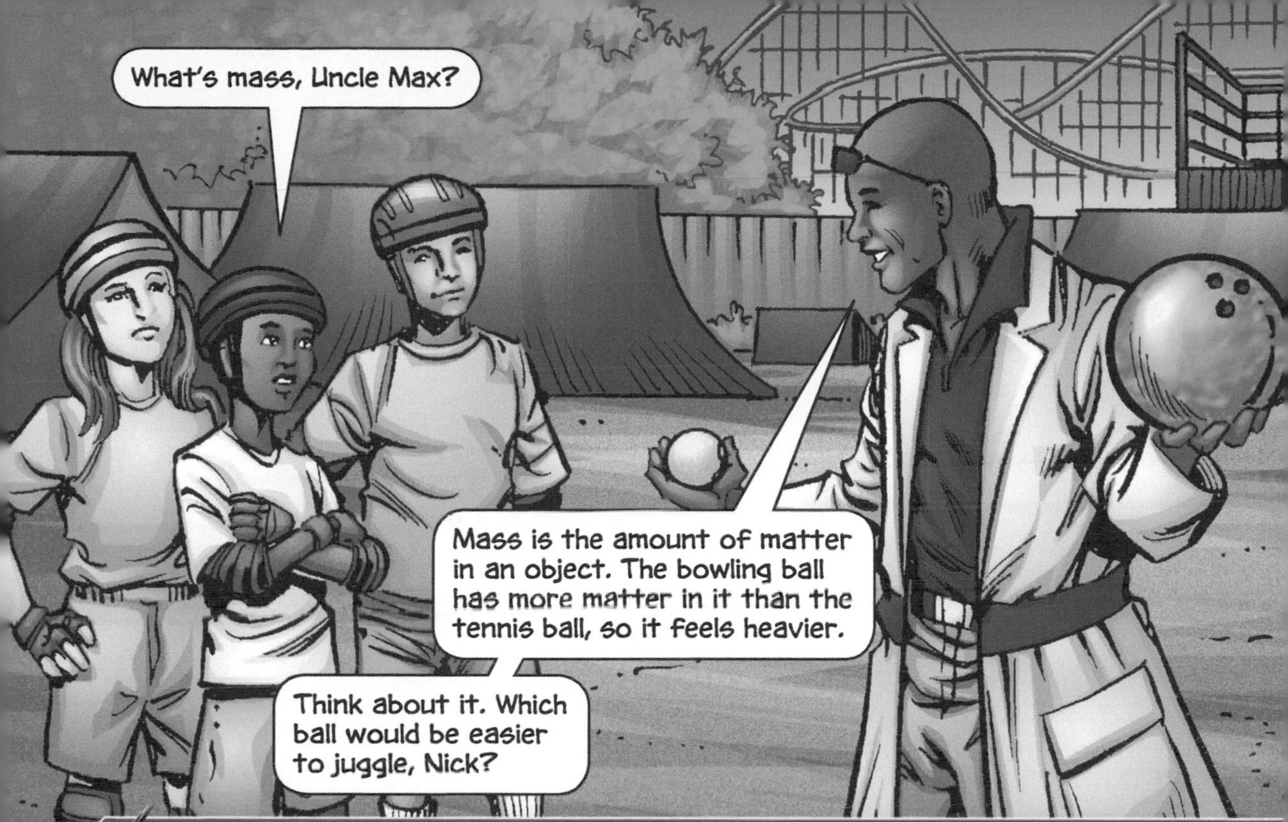
What's mass, Uncle Max?
Mass is the amount of matter in an object. The bowling ball has more matter in it than the tennis ball, so it feels heavier.
Think about it. Which ball would be easier to juggle, Nick?

GRAVITATIONAL PULL

ACCESS GRANTED: MAX AXIOM

Weight is different from mass. Weight is determined by gravity's pull on an object. Each planet in our solar system has a different gravitational pull. If you traveled to each of the places below, your mass would always be the same, but your weight would be different. Multiply your weight by the number shown below each planet to find out how much you would weigh there. If you weigh 100 pounds on Earth, you would weigh 38 pounds on Mars and 236 pounds on Jupiter.

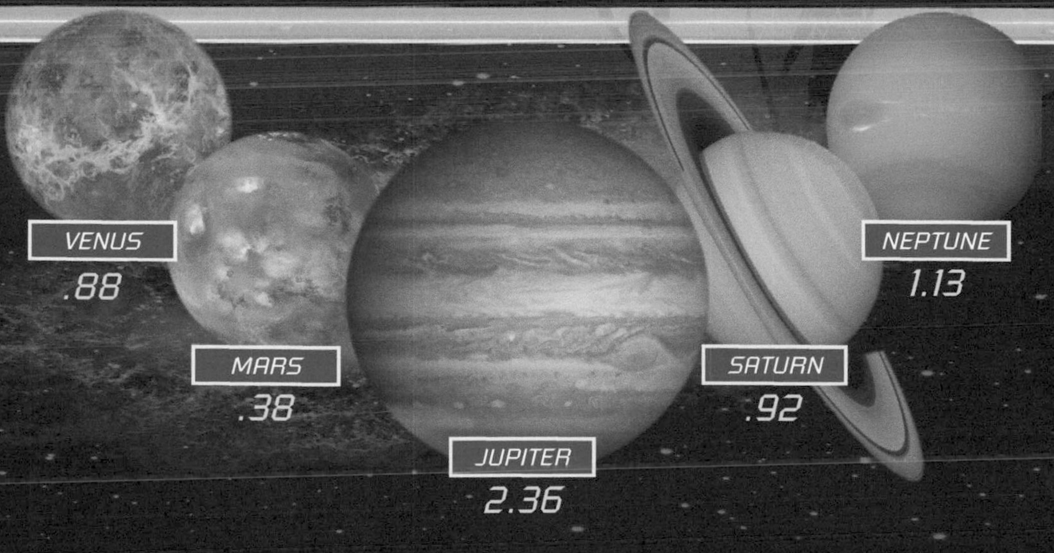
VENUS
.88
MARS
.38
JUPITER
2.36
SATURN
.92
NEPTUNE
1.13

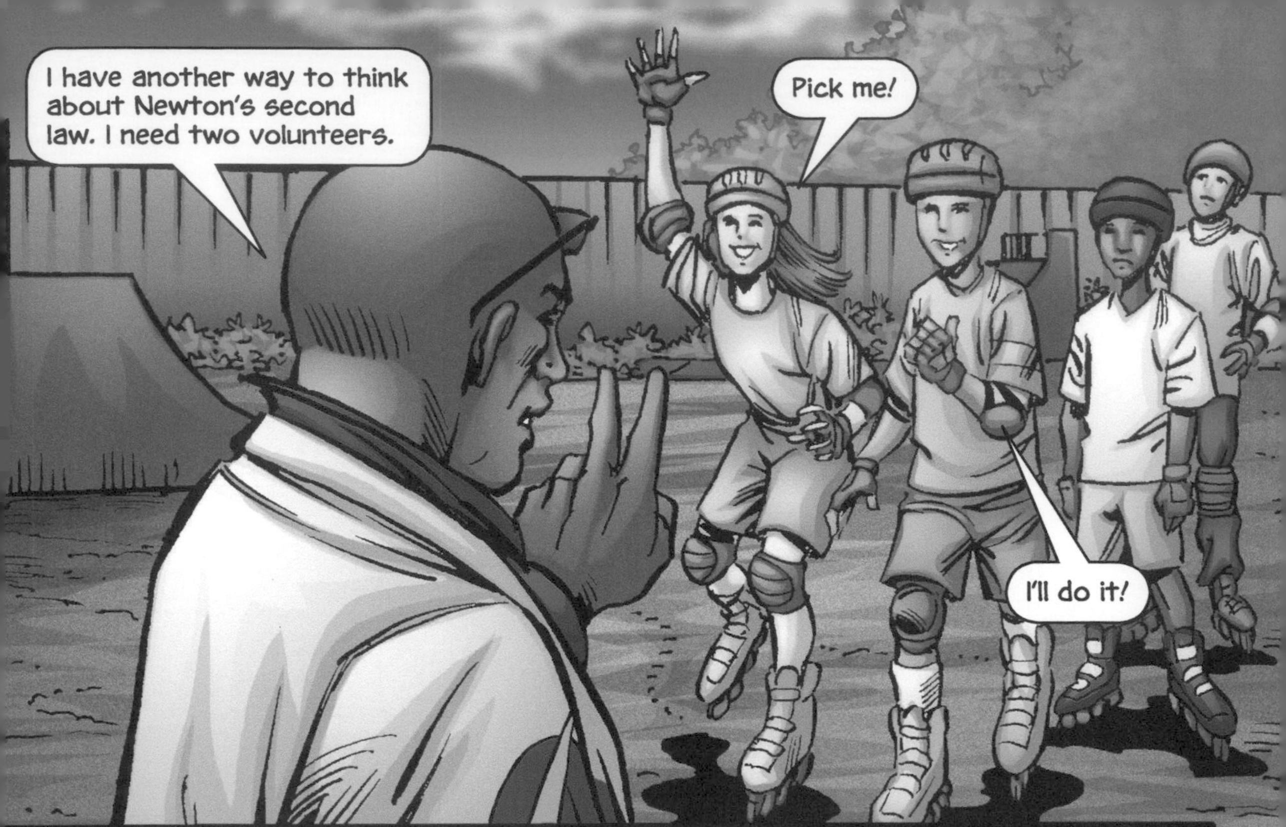
I have another way to think about Newton's second law. I need two volunteers.
Pick me!
I'll do it!

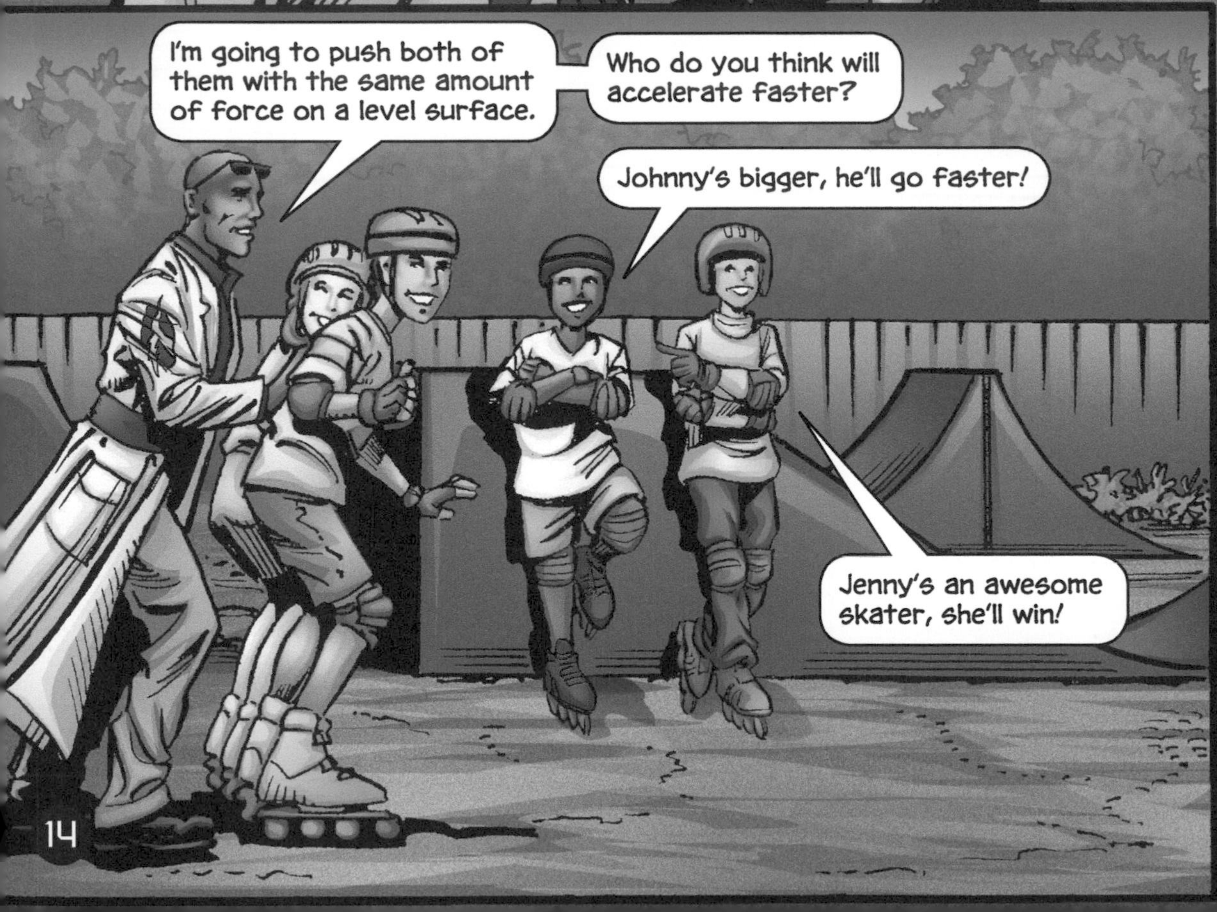
I'm going to push both of them with the same amount of force on a level surface.
Who do you think will accelerate faster?
Johnny's bigger, he'll go faster!
Jenny's an awesome skater, she'll win!

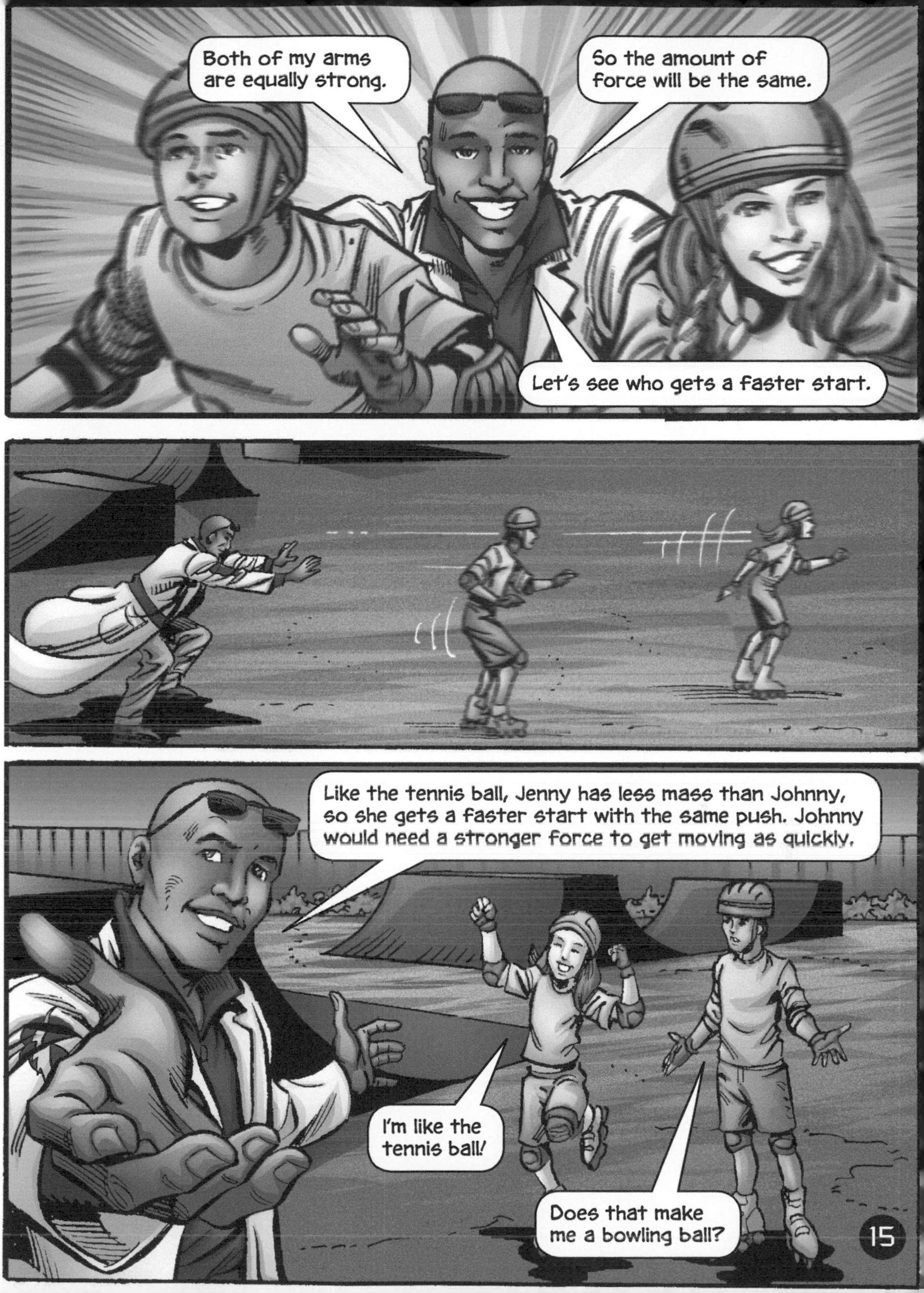
Both of my arms are equally strong.
So the amount of force will be the same.
Let's see who gets a faster start.
Like the tennis ball, Jenny has less mass than Johnny, so she gets a faster start with the same push. Johnny would need a stronger force to get moving as quickly.
I'm like the tennis ball!
Does that make me a bowling ball?

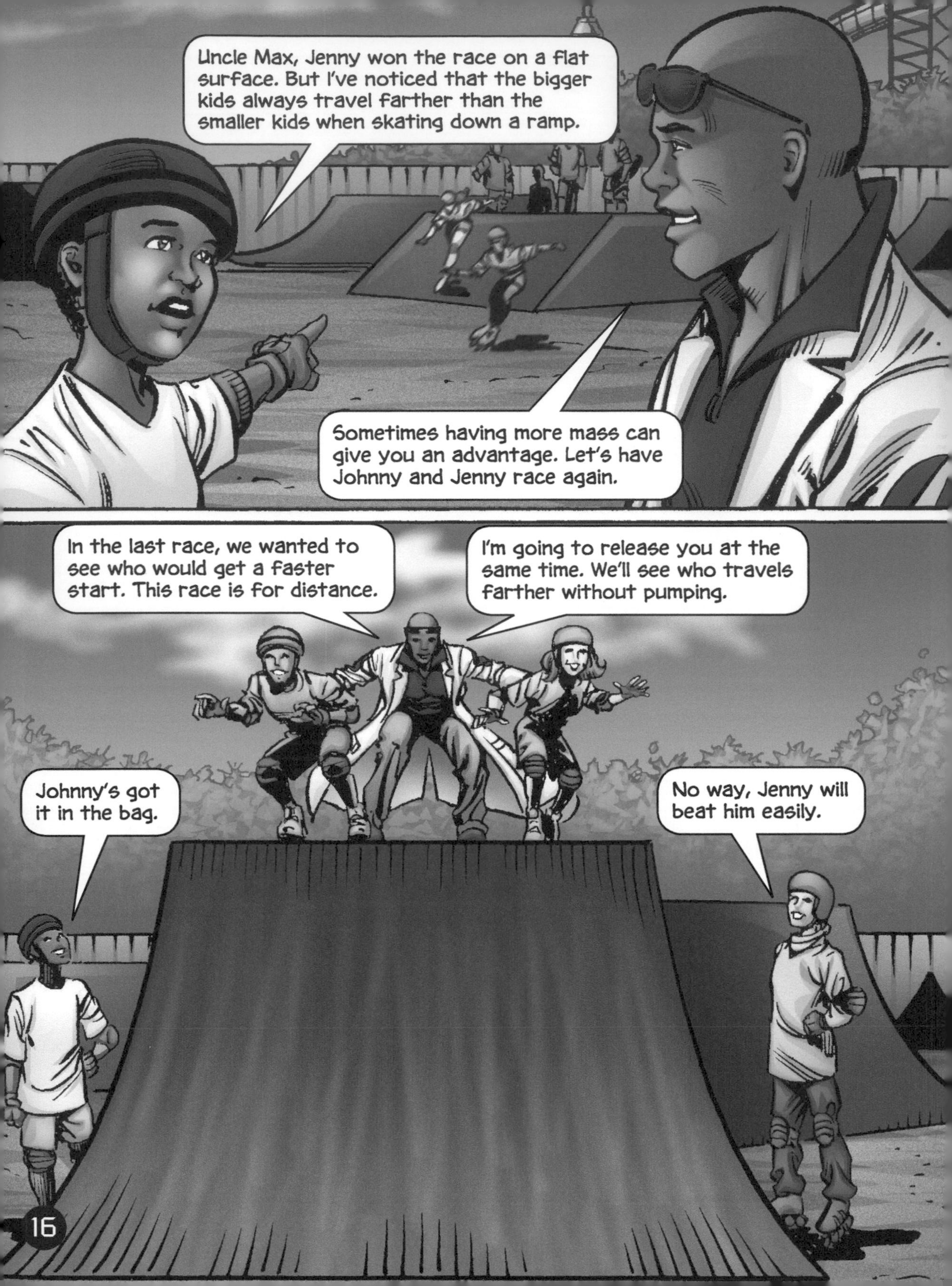
Uncle Max, Jenny won the race on a flat surface. But I've noticed that the bigger kids always travel farther than the smaller kids when skating down a ramp.
Sometimes having more mass can give you an advantage. Let's have Johnny and Jenny race again.
In the last race, we wanted to see who would get a faster start. This race is for distance.
I'm going to release you at the same time. We'll see who travels farther without pumping.
Johnny's got it in the bag.
No way, Jenny will beat him easily.

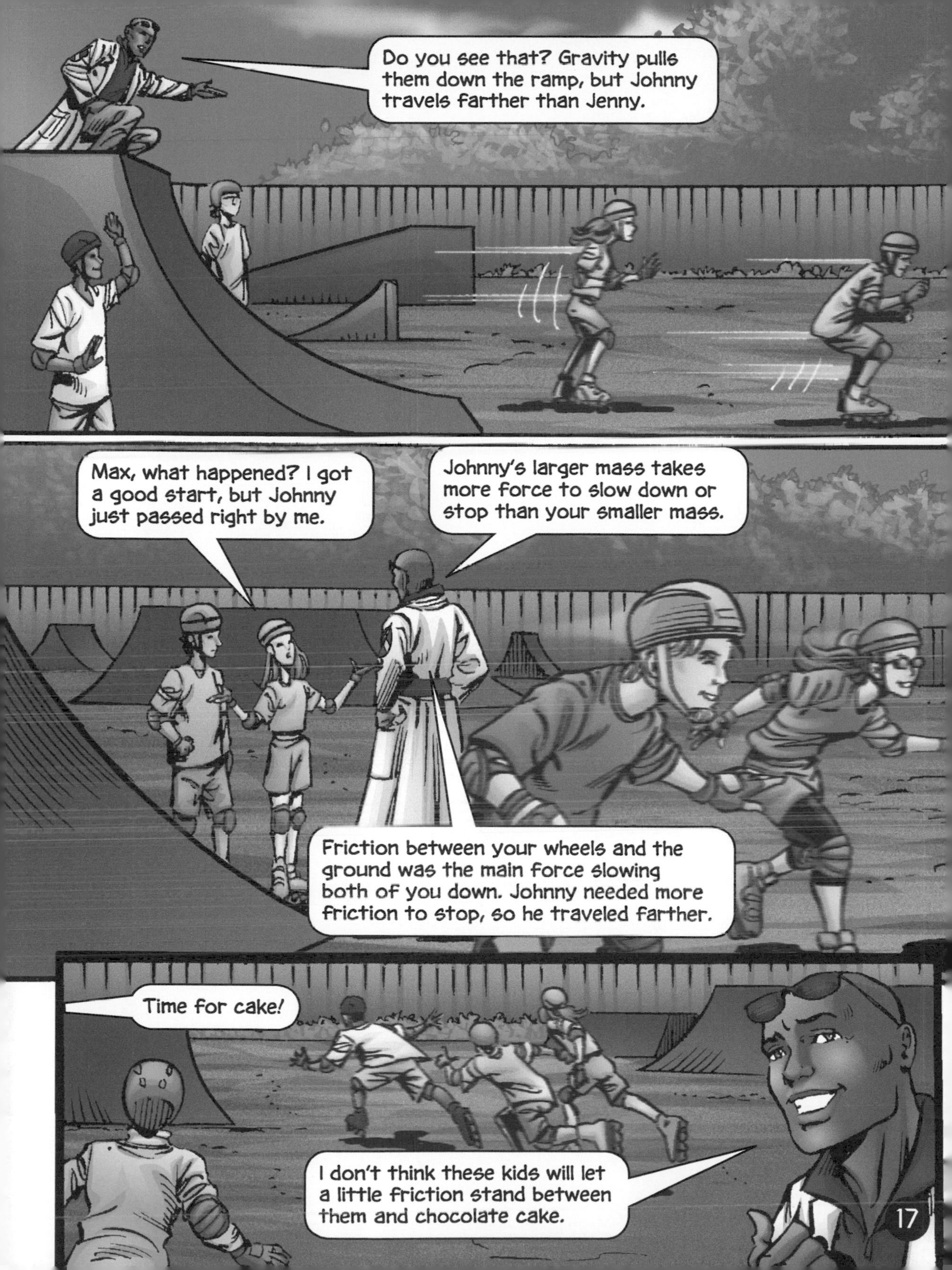

Do you see that? Gravity pulls them down the ramp, but Johnny travels farther than Jenny.
Max, what happened? I got a good start, but Johnny just passed right by me.
Johnny's larger mass takes more force to slow down or stop than your smaller mass.
Friction between your wheels and the ground was the main force slowing both of you down. Johnny needed more friction to stop, so he traveled farther.
Time for cake!
I don't think these kids will let a little friction stand between them and chocolate cake.

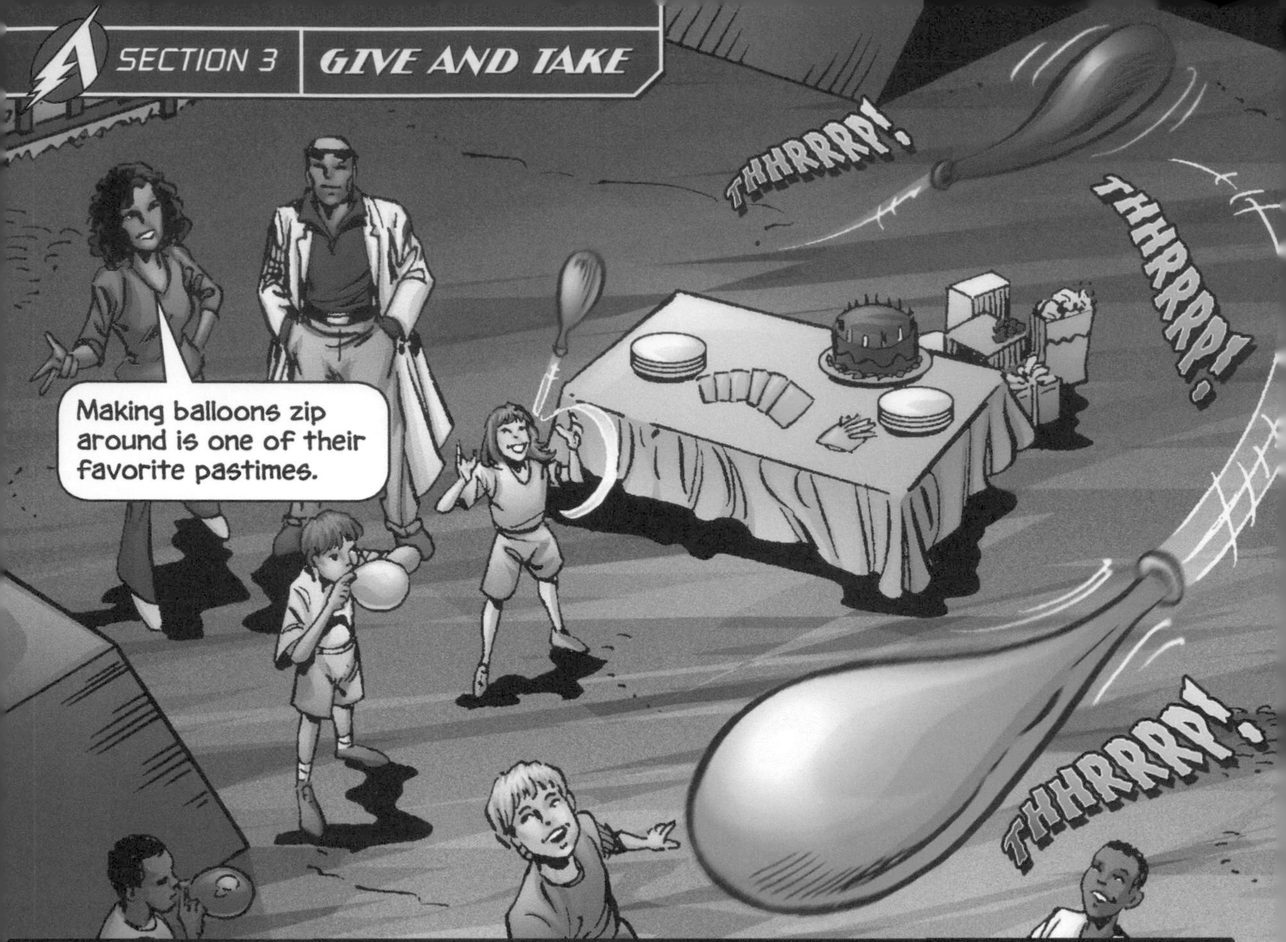
Making balloons zip around is one of their favorite pastimes.
THHRRRP!
THHRRRP!
THHRRRP!

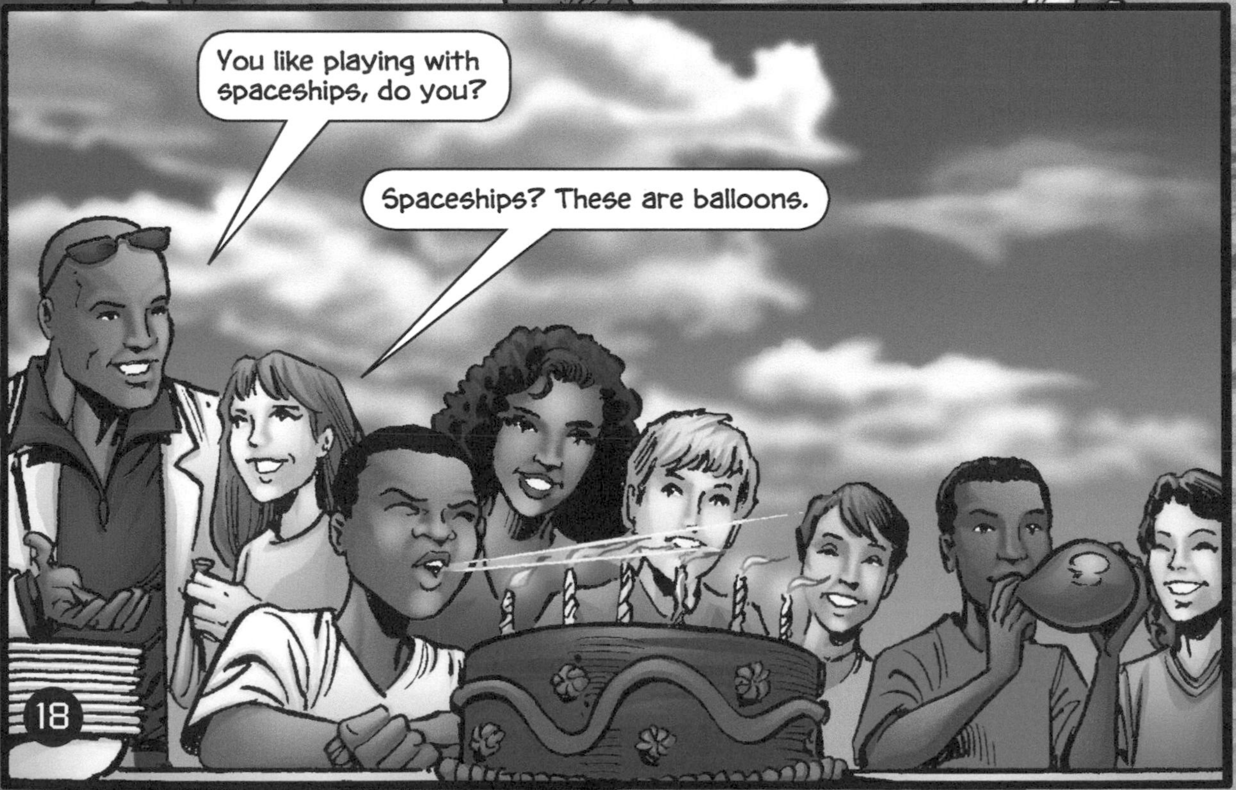
You like playing with spaceships, do you?
Spaceships? These are balloons.

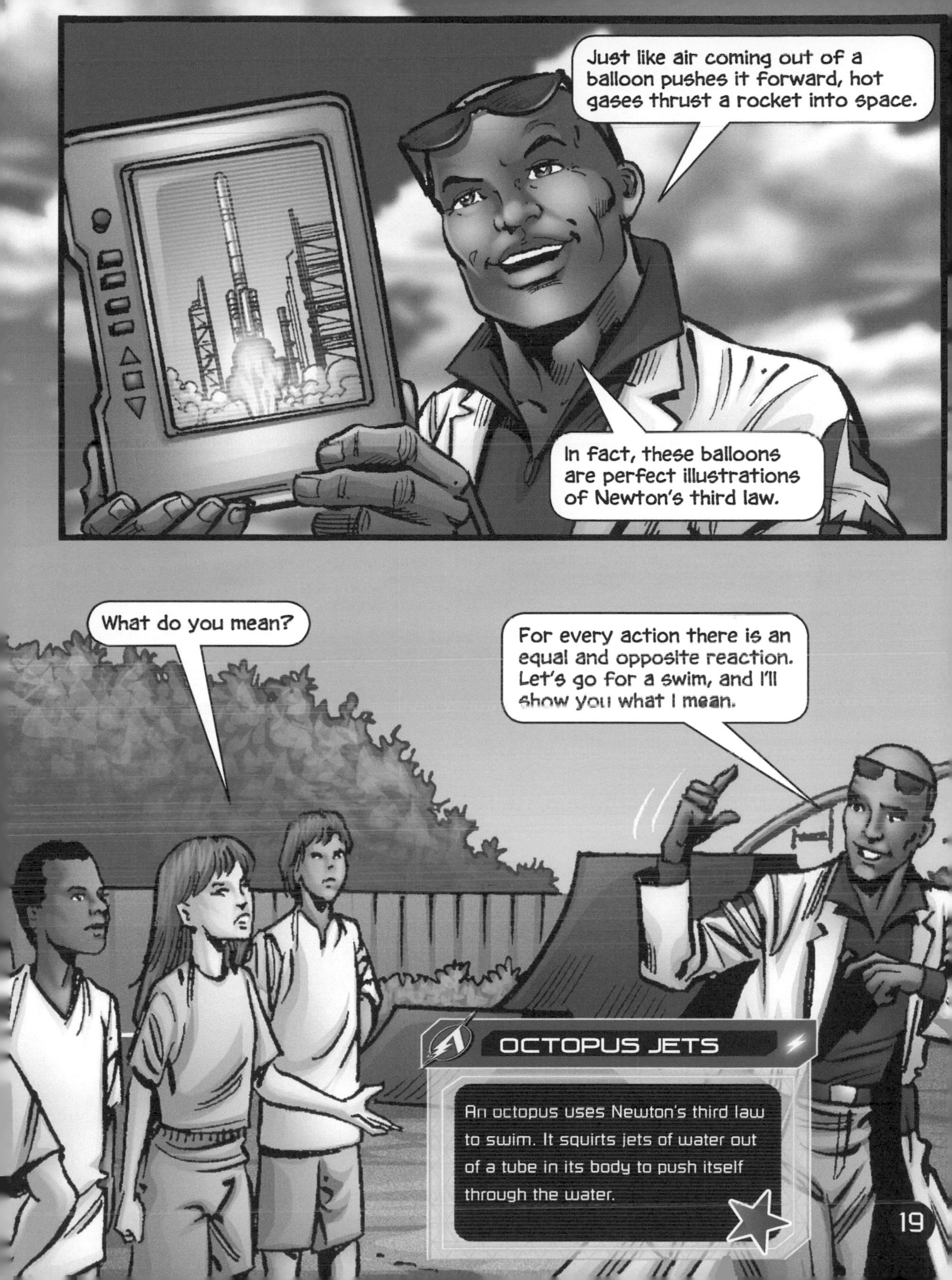
Just like air coming out of a balloon pushes it forward, hot gases thrust a rocket into space.
In fact, these balloons are perfect illustrations of Newton's third law.
What do you mean?
For every action there is an equal and opposite reaction. Let's go for a swim, and I'll show you what I mean.

OCTOPUS JETS

An octopus uses Newton's third law to swim. It squirts jets of water out of a tube in its body to push itself through the water.

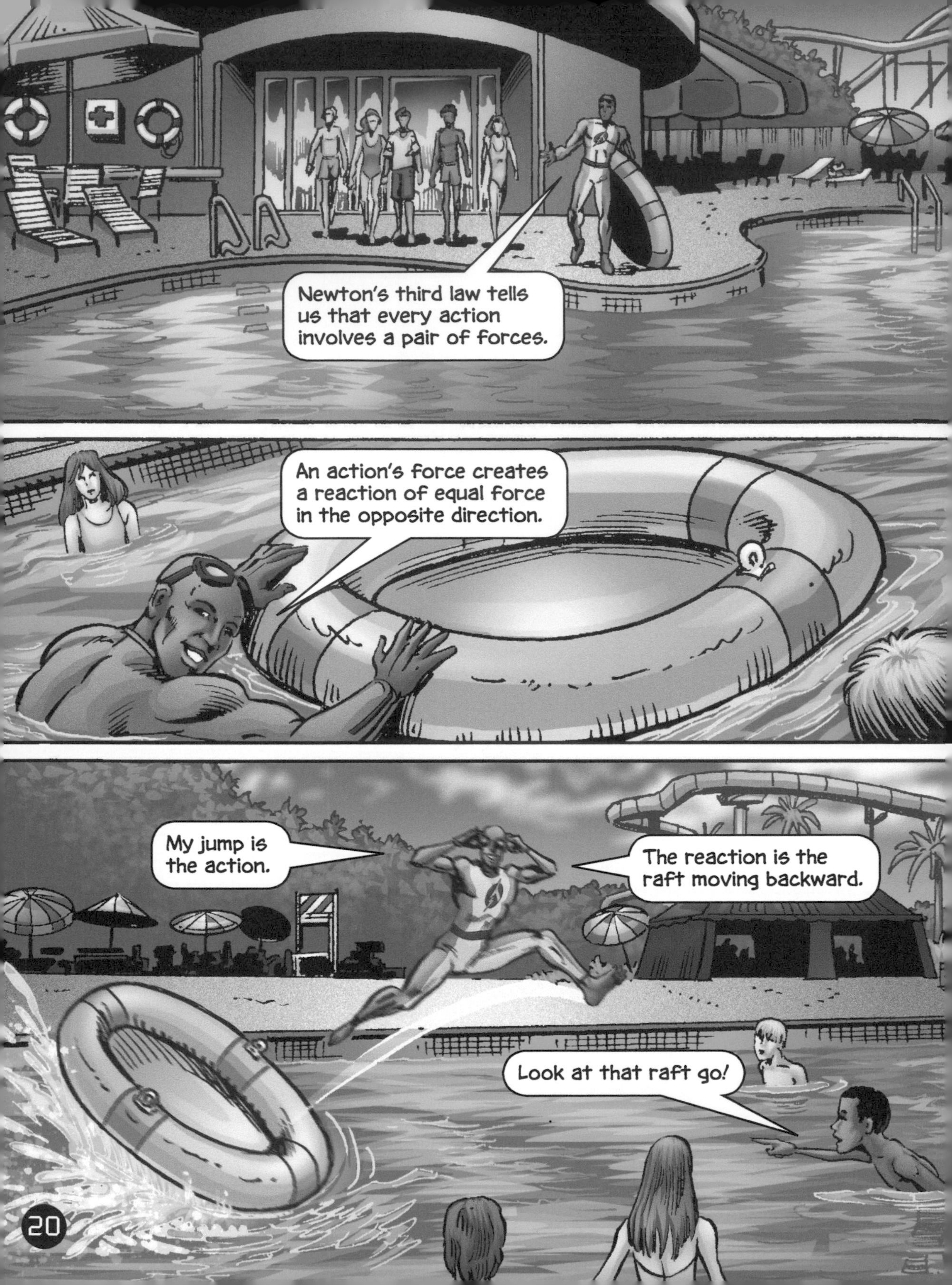

Newton's third law tells us that every action involves a pair of forces.
An action's force creates a reaction of equal force in the opposite direction.
My jump is the action.
The reaction is the raft moving backward.
Look at that raft go!

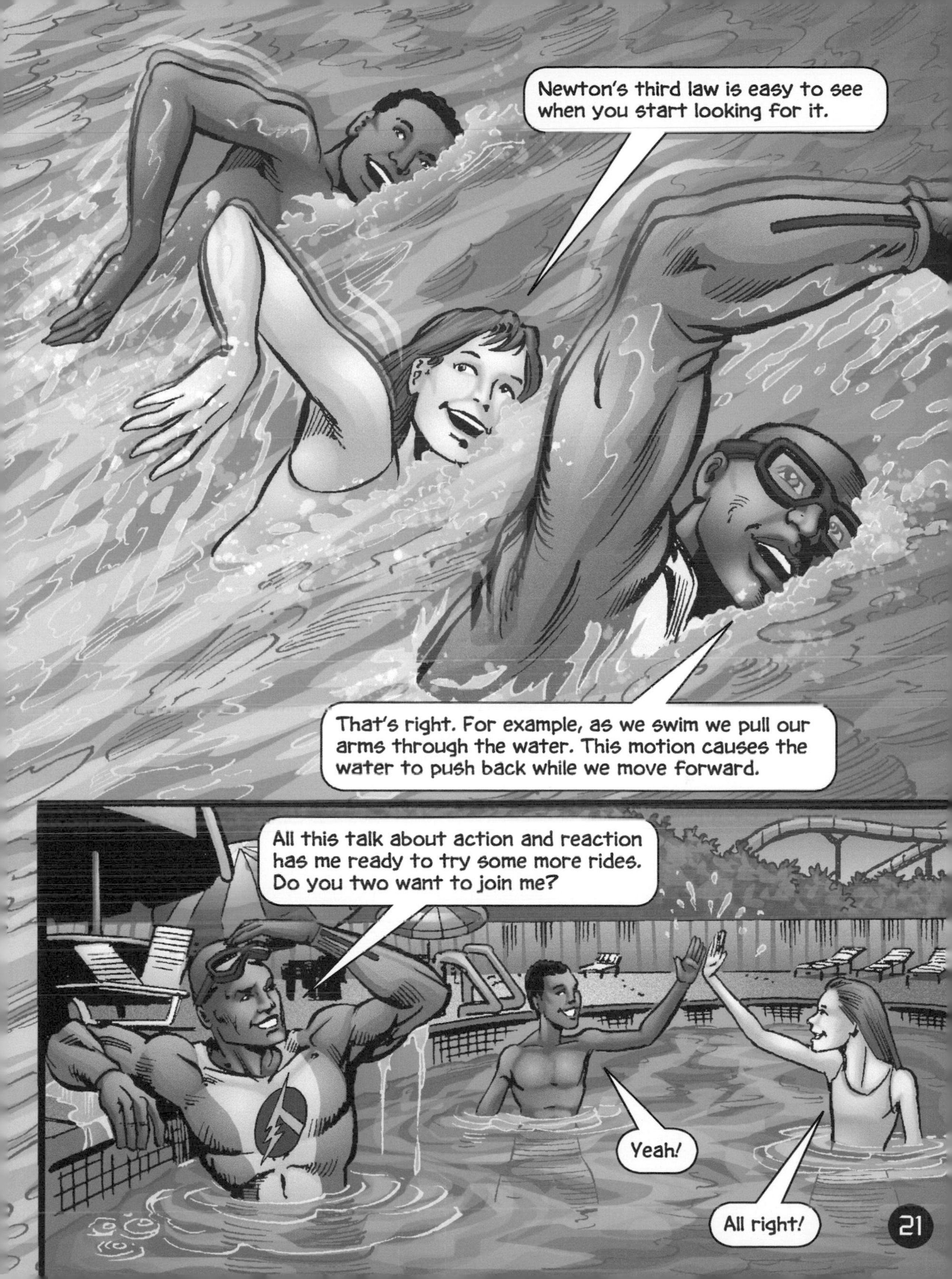
Newton's third law is easy to see when you start looking for it.
That's right. For example, as we swim we pull our arms through the water. This motion causes the water to push back while we move forward.
All this talk about action and reaction has me ready to try some more rides. Do you two want to join me?
Yeah!
All right!

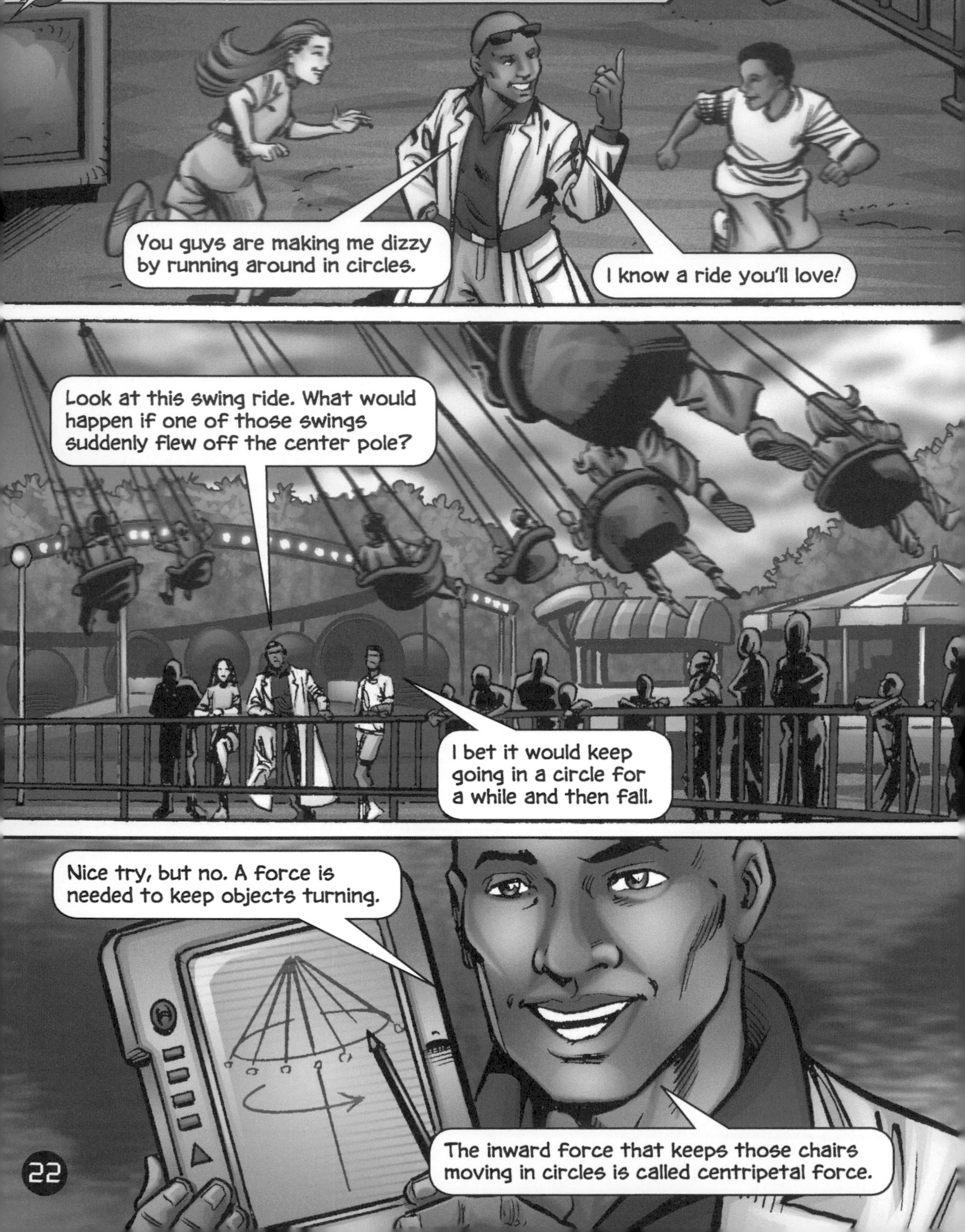
You guys are making me dizzy by running around in circles.
I know a ride you'll love!
Look at this swing ride. What would happen if one of those swings suddenly flew off the center pole?
I bet it would keep going in a circle for a while and then fall.
Nice try, but no. A force is needed to keep objects turning.
The inward force that keeps those chairs moving in circles is called centripetal force.

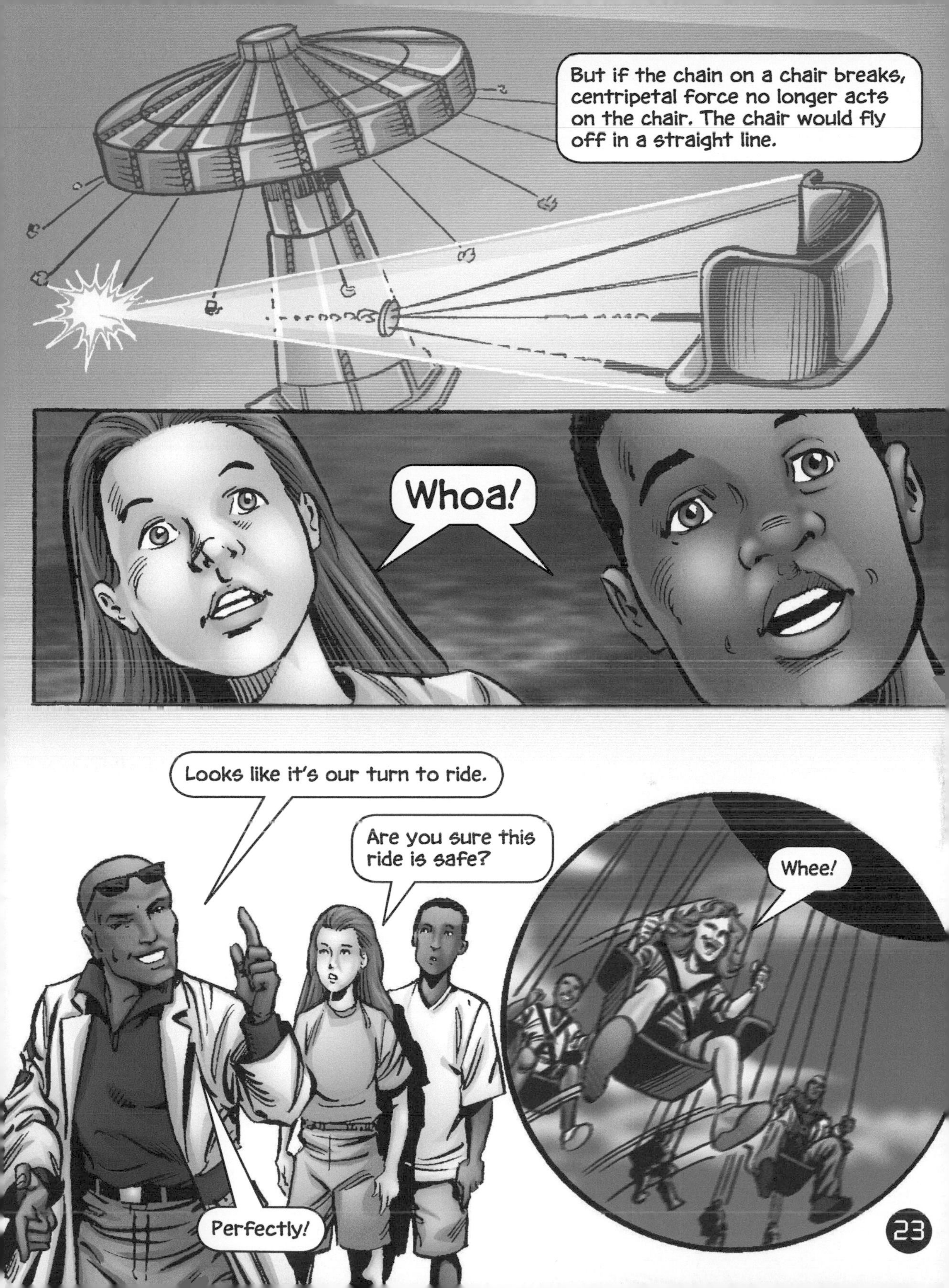
But if the chain on a chair breaks, centripetal force no longer acts on the chair. The chair would fly off in a straight line.
Whoa!
Looks like it's our turn to ride.
Are you sure this ride is safe?
Perfectly!
Whee!

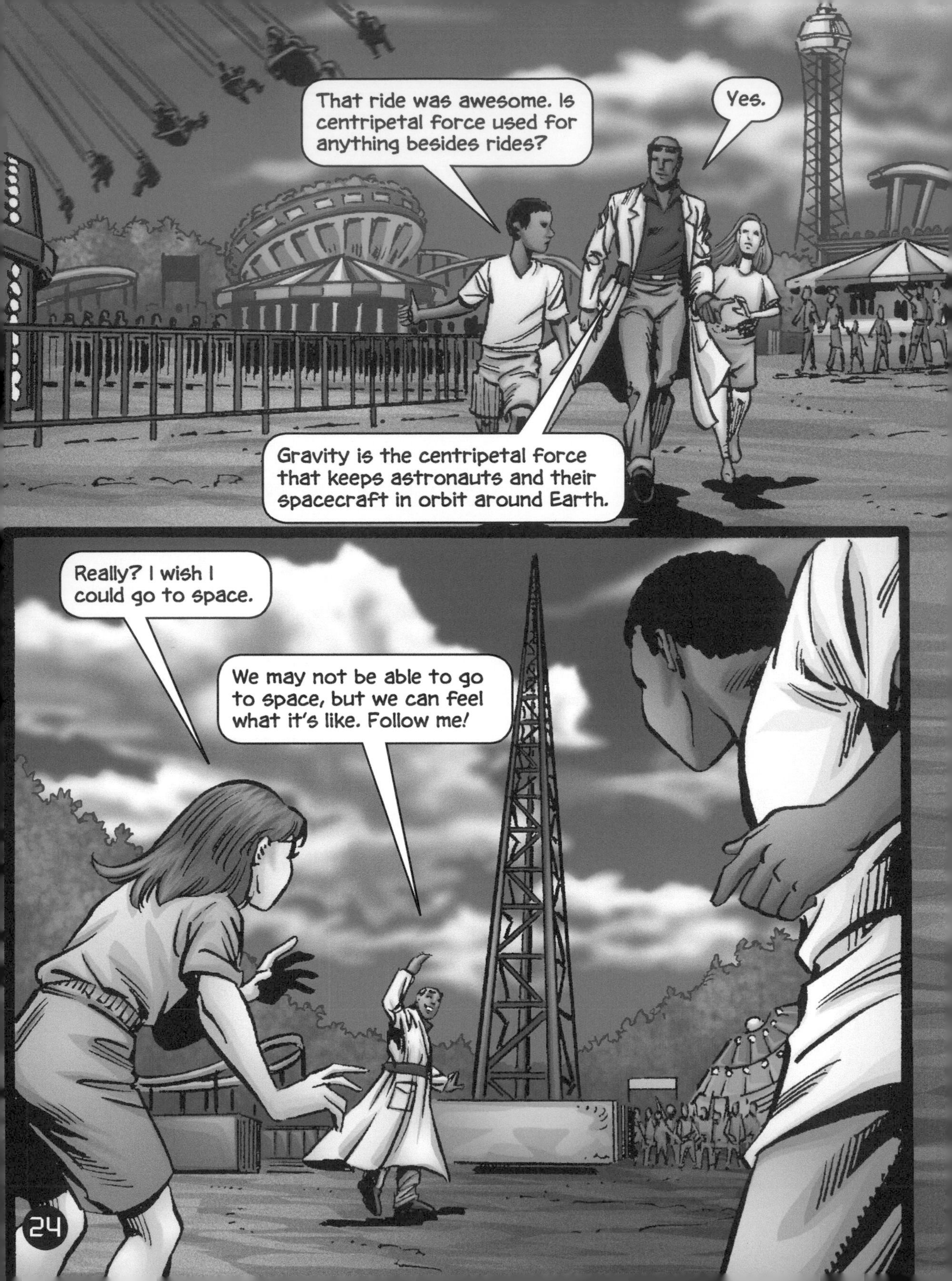
That ride was awesome. Is centripetal force used for anything besides rides?
Yes.
Gravity is the centripetal force that keeps astronauts and their spacecraft in orbit around Earth.
Really? I wish I could go to space.
We may not be able to go to space, but we can feel what it's like. Follow me!

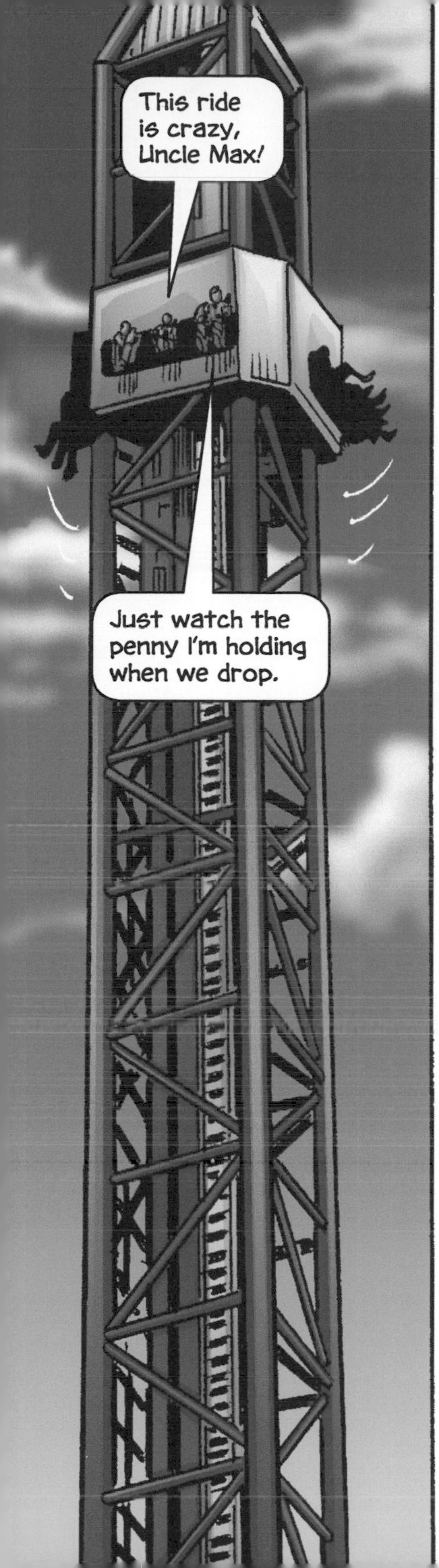
This ride is crazy, Uncle Max!
Just watch the penny I'm holding when we drop.

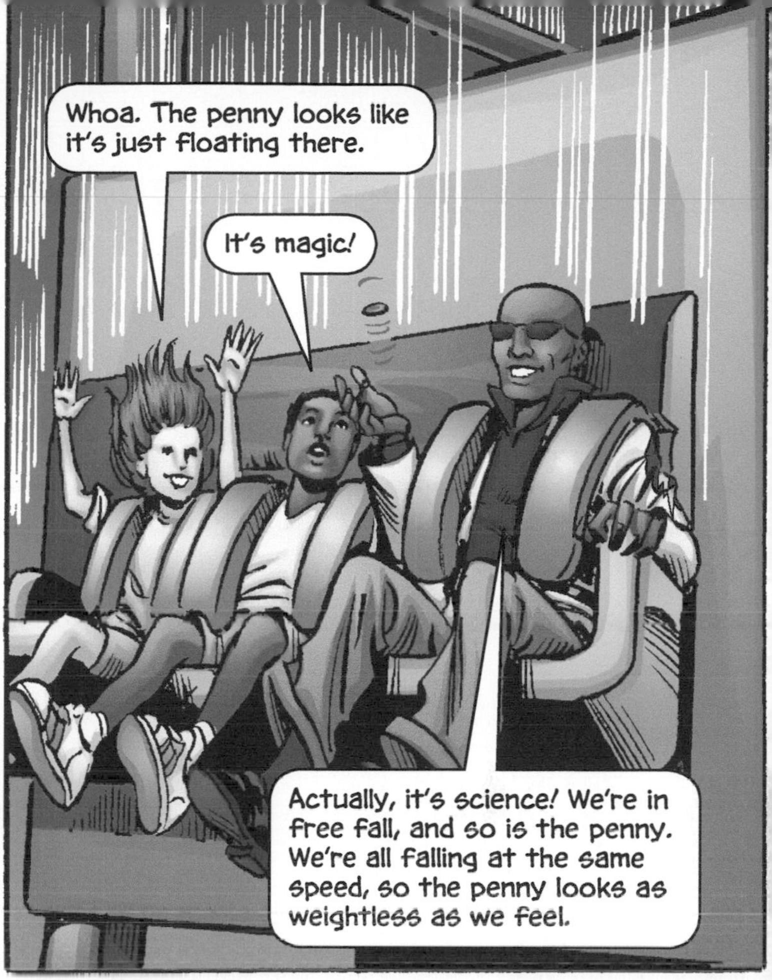
Whoa. The penny looks like it's just floating there.
It's magic!
Actually, it's science! We're in free fall, and so is the penny. We're all falling at the same speed, so the penny looks as weightless as we feel.

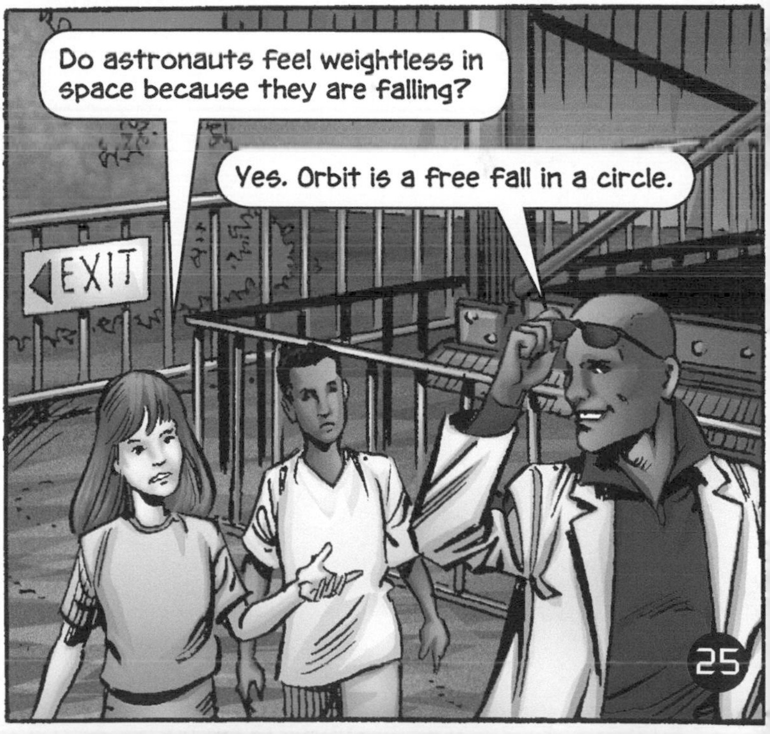
Do astronauts feel weightless in space because they are falling?
Yes. Orbit is a free fall in a circle.
EXIT

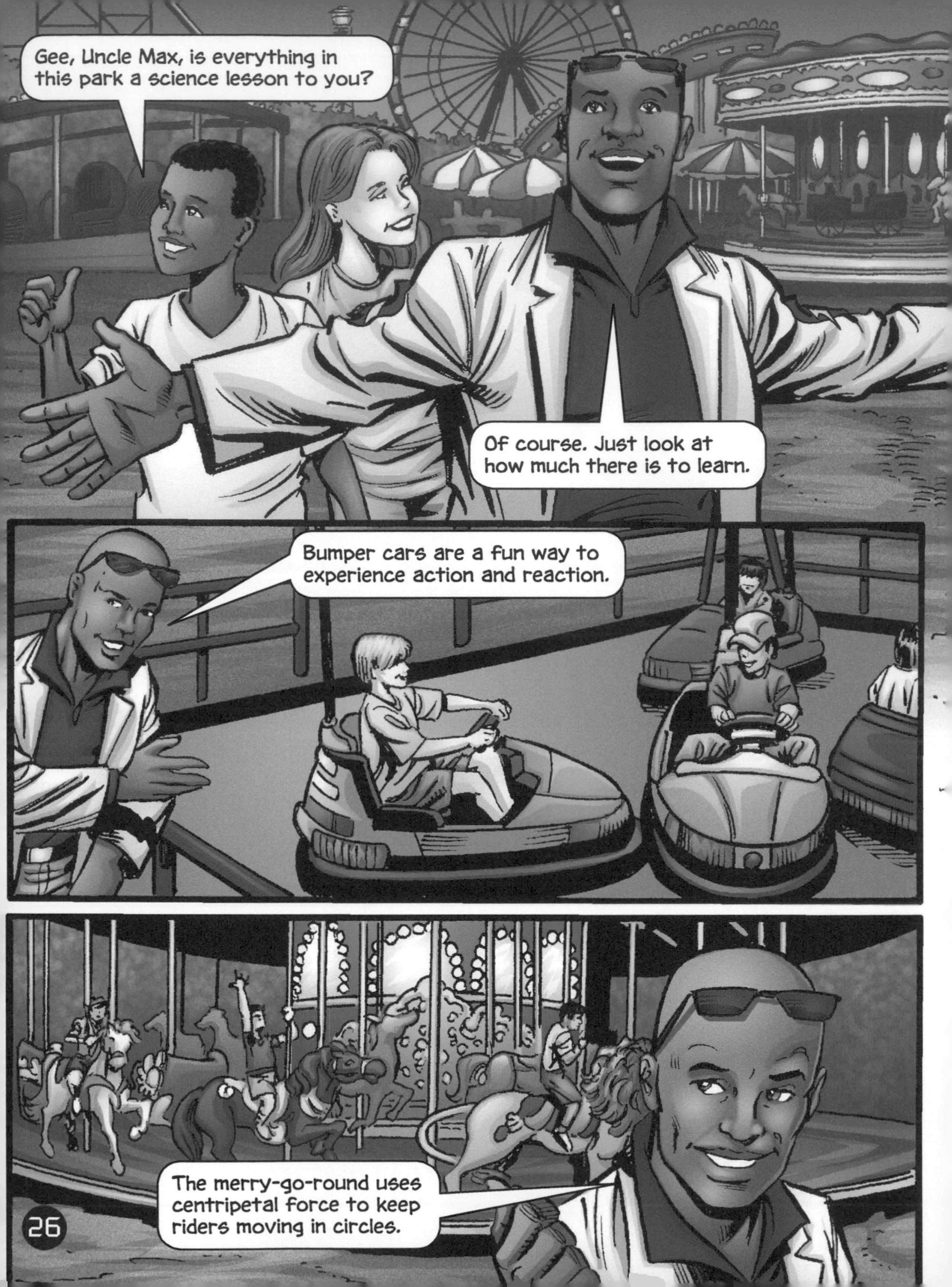

Gee, Uncle Max, is everything in this park a science lesson to you?
Of course. Just look at how much there is to learn.
Bumper cars are a fun way to experience action and reaction.
The merry-go-round uses centripetal force to keep riders moving in circles.

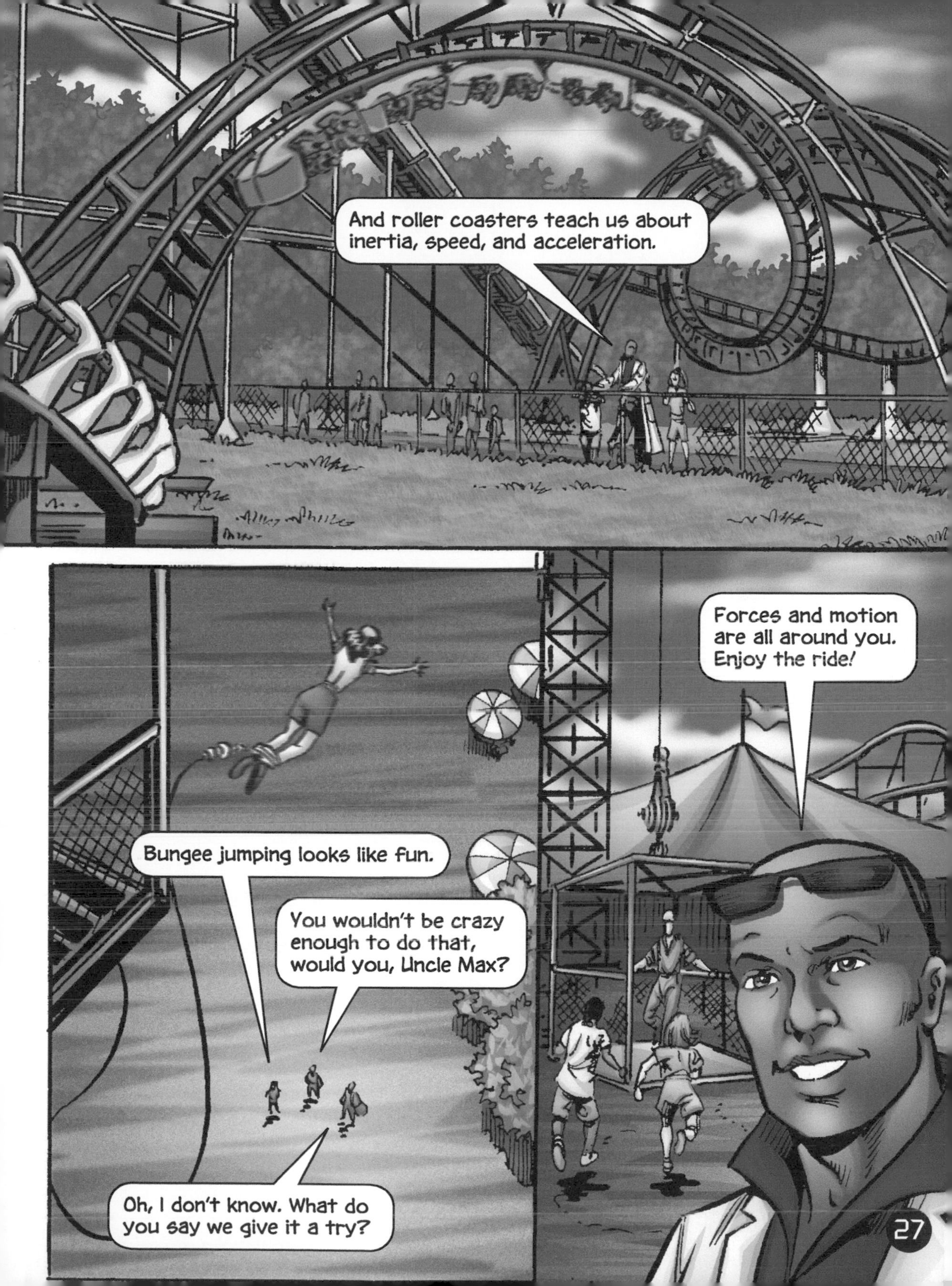

And roller coasters teach us about inertia, speed, and acceleration.
Bungee jumping looks like fun.
You wouldn't be crazy enough to do that, would you, Uncle Max?
Oh, I don't know. What do you say we give it a try?
Forces and motion are all around you. Enjoy the ride!

FORCES AND MOTION

To feel the most speed on a roller coaster, sit in the last seat. It reaches the top of the hills just as the front of the roller coaster gains its top speed down the hills.

The motion of amusement park rides sometimes makes you feel sick. Swinging, spinning, or going around in loops causes your eyes and the fluid in your ears to send confusing signals to your brain. Your brain can't decide which way is up or down.

Forces that don't cause objects to move are balanced forces. A great example of balanced forces is the chair you're sitting on. As you sit on a chair, the force of gravity pulls your body downward. At the same time, the chair pushes upward on your body with an equal force. Without these forces in balance, the chair would break and you would find yourself sitting on the ground.

Friction actually slows down skydivers as they fall from an airplane. Air resistance is a form of friction that happens between air and an object moving through it. Even with air resistance, skydivers reach speeds of about 120 miles (193 kilometers) per hour during free falls.

The peregrine falcon is the fastest animal on Earth. In a steep hunting dive, it can reach 200 miles (322 kilometers) per hour.

Inertia causes objects to stay at rest or keep moving until a force acts upon them. In a moving car, inertia can be dangerous. Your body moves at the same speed as the car. If the driver suddenly slams on the brakes, the car stops, but your body keeps moving forward. Your seat belt applies a force to stop your body's forward motion. It's the only thing that keeps you from flying through the windshield.

If you're looking for the fastest horse on the merry-go-round, pick an outside horse. To complete the circle, it must cover more distance in the same amount of time as an inside horse.

BALLOON CAR

Turn some candy into a sweet ride! Harness the power of motion to make it zoom forward!

WHAT YOU NEED:

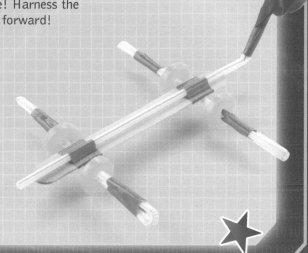

- small balloon
- flexible plastic straw
- flat wooden craft stick
- 2 straight plastic straws
- 4 round hard candies with holes in the middle
- tape
- measuring tape
- paper and pencil

WHAT YOU DO:

1. Stretch out the balloon so it is easier to inflate.

2. Put the short end of the flexible straw into the balloon.

3. Seal the mouth of the balloon around the end of the straw with tape.

4. Tape the straw to the top of your flat wooden stick. This is your "jet."

5. Slip two candies onto a straight straw. Bend back and tape the tips of the straw on both ends so the candies can't fall off. Repeat with the second straw.

6. Tape the straws with the candies to the bottom of the flat stick. One should be directly below the balloon. These are your "wheels." Make sure they spin freely.

7. Blow up the balloon through the straw. Put your finger over the end of the straw to keep the air from escaping.

8. Place your car on a smooth surface. Bend the flexible end of the straw so the balloon doesn't touch the ground.

9. Release your finger from the straw and let the car go. Measure how far it goes and record the data.

10. See if you can find ways to change how fast or slow the car goes. Make a ramp or add weight to your car to see how it impacts its speed. Note what you change and record your measurements each time you modify your car.

DISCUSSION QUESTIONS

1. Newton's third law of motion says that every action has an equal and opposite reaction. Which amusement park ride is the best example of Newton's third law—the roller coaster, the swings, or the bumper cars? Why?

2. How does a roller coaster stop at the end of a ride? What forces are at work to help it stop?

3. Newton's first law of motion states that an object at rest stays at rest. Why does a ball roll? Why does a ball eventually stop rolling?

4. Imagine three jugglers. One juggles golf balls, one juggles tennis balls, and the third juggles small foam balls. Which juggler would use the greatest force to juggle? Explain why you think your choice is correct.

5. Speed and acceleration are both tied to how fast something moves. What are the differences between them?

WRITING PROMPTS

1. What is a force? Write a definition for force with your own words based on what you read in the book.

2. When a moving roller coaster car stops, what happens to its passengers? Write a short paragraph about a time you rode a roller coaster or a different amusement park ride. Describe what it felt like when the ride came to a stop.

3. Magnetism is a kind of force. Write a short paragraph explaining the force magnets exert on other objects.

4. Centripetal force is an inward force that keeps things moving in a circular path. Max describes a circular chair swing ride as using centripetal force. Write about a time outside an amusement park where you encountered a centripetal force.

TAKE A QUIZ! ☆